Soliloquy № 7

Addressing Hidden Influences
That Quietly Erode Church Leaders

chris mcGough

XULON PRESS

SOLILOQUY № 7 Copyright © 2020 by Christopher M. McGough.

All rights reserved. No part of this book may be reproduced, stored in or introduced into a retrieval system, or transmitted, in any form or by any means (electronic, mechanical, photocopying, recording or otherwise), without the prior written permission of the copyright owner, except by a reviewer who may quote brief passages in a review. For more information, address: Xulon Press, 2301 Lucien Way, Suite 415, Maitland, FL 32751.

This book is sold subject to the condition that it shall not, by way of trade or otherwise, be lent, re-sold, hired out or otherwise circulated without the author's prior consent in any form of binding or cover other than that in which it is published and without a similar condition including this condition being imposed on the subsequent purchaser.

Library of Congress Cataloging-in-Publication Data

Names: McGough, Chris, author.

Title: Soliloquy № 7: Addressing Hidden Influences That Quietly Erode Church Leaders / Chris McGough

Description: Florida : Xulon, 2020.

Includes bibliographical references.

978-1-6628-0111-2 (Ebook) | 978-1-6628-0110-5 (hardcover) | 978-1-6628-0109-9 (paperback)

Subjects: LCSH : Religion/Christian Living/Leadership & Mentoring

LC record available at https://lccn.loc.gov/

First hardcover edition November 2020

First paperback edition November 2020

Book design by Chris McGough

Jacket designed by Chris McGough

Author photograph by Kyelah McGough

Unless otherwise indicated, all Scripture quotations in this publication are taken from the ESV® Bible (The Holy Bible, English Standard Version®), copyright © 2001 by Crossway, a publishing ministry of Good News Publishers. Used by permission. All rights reserved.

Also used: Holy Bible, Contemporary English Version® (CEV). Copyright © 1991, 1992, 1995 by American Bible Society, Used by permission;

Also used: Complete Jewish Bible (CJB). Copyright © 1998 by David H. Stern. All rights reserved. Used by permission;

Also used: The Expanded Bible (EXB). Copyright ©2011 by Thomas Nelson. Used by permission. All rights reserved.

Also used: Holy Bible: International Standard Version® (ISV). Copyright © 1996-forever by The ISV Foundation. ALL RIGHTS RESERVED INTERNATIONALLY. Used by permission;

Also used: Fire Bible Student Edition; New International Version® (NIV). Copyright © 2007 by Life International Publishers;

Also used: Holy Bible, New Living Translation® (NLT). Copyright ©1996, 2004, 2015 by Tyndale House Foundation. Used by permission of Tyndale House Publishers, a Division of Tyndale House Ministries, Carol Stream, Illinois 60188. All rights reserved;

Also used: The Passion Translation® (TPT). Copyright © 2017, 2018 by Passion & Fire Ministries, Inc. Used by permission. All rights reserved. ThePassionTranslation.com;

Also used: The Voice™ (VOICE). Copyright © 2012 by Ecclesia Bible Society. Used by permission. All rights reserved.

First Edition

Printed in the United States of America

While the author has made every effort to provide accurate Internet addresses and other contact information at the time of publication, neither the publisher nor the author assumes any responsibility for errors, or for changes that occur after publication. Further, the publisher does not have any control over and does not assume any responsibility for author or third-party websites or their content.

Published by Xulon Press 2301 Lucien Way, Suite 415 Maitland, FL 32751

soliloquynumberseven.com

24 23 22 21 20 10 9 8 7 6 5 4 3 2 1

This book is dedicated to my dad:

*Thanks for the Years of
Unselfish & Quiet Obedience to the Lord and for
Immersing in a Lifetime
Of Service to Him.*

*Now Unburdened Miles Beyond Earth...Rest.
Your Supportive & Encouraging Voice
Echoes Non-stop.*

(Max McGough, 1947-2015)

...and to the current & future church/ministry leaders
that work to equip God's people to minister
to the world and make disciples,
and that help to prepare the bride of Christ
to meet our soon-returning Groom.

Sehnsucht

"Can you see the man of your family who [thinks he] has more talent in his little finger than all the rest in their united brains...?"

—Charles Dickens, *Martin Chuzzlewit*

CONTENTS

Introduction 1

1 The Ocean's Deep Secret
   Guarding Your Heart & the Survivor Bias.......... 17

2 Fashion Statements
   Avoiding Deceitful Communication & Enclothed
   Cognition 39
   Clothing Layer #1: Base Layer
   Clothing Layer #2: Mid-Layer
   Clothing Layer #3: Outer Layer

3 Architects of the Archetype
   Fixating on Purpose & the Swimmer's Body Illusion 107
   Construction Phase #1: Foundation
   Construction Phase #2: Framing
   Construction Phase #3: Exterior
   Construction Phase #4: Interior

4 Desert Sand Through the Hourglass
   Staying on the Path & the Black Swan Theory 165
   Cairn Marker #1: A Mirage in the Desert
   Cairn Marker #2: Desert Sage

5 Altogether Separate
   Deviating from the Standard & the Conformity Bias 203

Conclusion 225
Terms & Definitions 231
Appendix: Cognitive Bias Charts 235
Acknowledgements 239
A Note on Sources 241
About the Author 265

Soliloquy № 7

INTRODUCTION

"A prince who is not himself wise cannot be wisely advised...Good advice depends on the shrewdness of the prince who seeks it, and not the shrewdness of the prince on good advice."

—Niccolò Machiavelli, *The Prince*

During his lifetime, Solomon—the wisest man to have ever lived—spoke 3,000 proverbs.[1] People came from every nation to hear his wisdom.[2] We know it was God who gave Solomon this incredible wisdom,[3] but he also had another source of wisdom that often gets overlooked. Solomon reveals that source to us: "When I was a son with my father, tender, the only one in the sight of my mother, he taught me and said to me, 'Let your heart hold fast to my words; and keep my commandments, and live.'"[4] Solomon's father, David, gave him words of wisdom that would give him life.

Solomon wrote down the same commands that David, his father, had given to him. Important people were coming from

---

1. 1 Kings 4:32
2. 2 Chronicles 9:23
3. 2 Chronicles 1:7-12
4. Proverbs 4:3-4

faraway places "seeking the presence of Solomon, to hear the wisdom which God had put in his heart."[1] Meanwhile, Solomon was writing down his wisdom addressed to his own son. He knew that it was important to pass down these life-giving commands to the next generation as this wisdom was given to him. These commands would safeguard his son's life and keep him from the path of destruction.

In the first seven chapters of Proverbs, Solomon admonishes his son with his wisdom in ten written soliloquies.[2] A *soliloquy* is a type of extended speech that's not given directly to another person; there's no one around to hear the speech. It's typically a speech that's given to no one in particular, or delivered to an audience as if there's no one around to hear the speech. These ten speeches that Solomon gave are full of life-giving commands.

I'm sure that Solomon verbally taught his son the wisdom in these soliloquies and didn't just write them down for him to read later. It seems, however, that Solomon wrote down his wisdom for more than just his son to know. He wanted the reader of his wisdom to really understand that this information was important to know.

There's no better way to convey the importance of this wisdom than to write as if he were speaking with his own son. Someone he cared for more than just anybody. Someone who would one day take his place as King of Israel. While Solomon's speeches might have been addressed to his son, Solomon was delivering these messages to everyone who would read what he had written.

In this book, we'll be using the seventh of Solomon's ten soliloquies—*Soliloquy № 7*—to discover five life-giving

---

1. 2 Chronicles 9:23

2. (1) Proverbs 1, (2) Proverbs 2, (3) Proverbs 3:1-12, (4) Proverbs 3:13-35, (5) Proverbs 4:1-9, (6) Proverbs 4:10-19, (7) Proverbs 4:20-27, (8) Proverbs 5, (9) Proverbs 6:20-25, (10) Proverbs 7.

lessons for church leaders. These lessons will help us as church leaders to focus on a few particularly important aspects of our lives that, if ignored, can erode the effectiveness of our lives and ministries over time. We find the seventh soliloquy in Proverbs 4:20-27. I've identified and numbered the five lessons within the verse [bold emphasis mine]:

> Listen carefully, my dear child, to everything that I teach you, and pay attention to all that I have to say. Fill your thoughts with my words until they penetrate deep into your spirit. Then, as you unwrap my words, they will impart true life and radiant health into the very core of your being.
>
> 1. So above all, **guard the affections of your heart**, for they affect all that you are. Pay attention to the welfare of your innermost being, for from there flows the wellspring of life.
> 2. **Avoid dishonest speech and pretentious words.** Be free from using perverse words no matter what!
> 3. Set your gaze on the path before you. **With fixed purpose, looking straight ahead**, ignore life's distractions.
> 4. Watch where you are going! **Stick to the path** of truth, and the road will be safe and smooth before you.
> 5. **Don't allow yourself to be sidetracked** for even a moment or take the detour that leads to darkness. (TPT)

As you can see, this one admonishment supplies five key life-giving lessons for the reader to ponder. Solomon's purpose was to teach his son to cling to the truth of God's Word, to live a life that stayed on the straight and narrow path, and to submit to God's Will instead of pursuing his own desires. We as ministry and church leaders can use Solomon's five commands to draw out instruction that will bring radiant health to our own lives and ministries.

FROM THE LEADER TO THE LEARNER

God gave the following instructions to the Levites who were responsible for ministering in the tabernacle:

> From twenty-five years old and upward they shall come to do duty in the service of the tent of meeting. And from the age of fifty years they shall withdraw from the duty of the service and serve no more. They minister to their brothers in the tent of meeting by keeping guard, but they shall do no service.[1]

While I'm not a Levite, I'm not under the old covenant, and I'm not quite fifty years of age, I have been a leader engaged in full-time church ministry for the past twenty-six years (at the time of this book's publication) and a Pastor's kid actively engaged in church ministry with my family since I was born. These years have provided me with wisdom that substantiates what I want to say to current and future church leaders. If you're currently preparing to minister in the church, or have been serving as a leader in the church or some other ministry for years, this book is for you.

I'm presently serving leaders in the church through my role as a professor at a private Christian university where I

---

1. Numbers 8:24-26

teach courses in youth ministry and church leadership. Having seen an alarming number of my friends who attended Bible college with me lose their focus and effectiveness in ministry, quit, and even fall away from their faith altogether, I've felt an urgency to "minister to my brothers in the tent of meeting by keeping guard." This includes both those presently engaged in ministry and my students whom I am preparing to enter full-time ministry.

There are five fundamental principles that I feel need to be guarded and slippery slopes that need to be illuminated. If these five principles are neglected, forgotten, or mishandled, it can affect church leaders in unintended but harmful ways over the course of ministry. The conversations I want to have with you, the reader, will include perspectives other than what is currently being held in the mainstream of church leadership and forming the ideology of many church leaders—and to which you may currently subscribe.

Perspective

My dad was a full-time pastor in the church for over forty-eight years before he went to be with Jesus in 2015. He had preached God's Word and ministered to people until cancer prevented him from continuing to do so. While he directly taught me these same lessons that Solomon taught to his son, I also saw each of them in action in my dad's life. This has directly influenced my own life and ministry. My dad was no David, and I am no Solomon, but the One who gives wisdom to those who ask for it can do so through both "show and tell." The key is for us to have our eyes and ears open as Solomon had urged his son to do— "Listen carefully…and pay attention."[1]

---

1. Proverbs 4:20

Soliloquy № 7

I realize that you and I may come from quite different places in ministry. We're likely to have different perspectives on the information that is in this book. I, too, once held a distinct perspective from those of my dad and other church leaders who through the years have helped to shape my perspectives.

Some who read this book may need to have their currently-held perspectives *challenged* in some ways. If you are seeking wisdom from God, he may use something said in this book to recalibrate the direction of your thinking. I will leave the challenging part up to the Holy Spirit as he knows where those exact areas in your life are located.

Others who read this book may need to have their perspectives *expanded*. It is unlikely that we've viewed a topic from every angle. To have a clearer understanding, we need to view issues from a variety of perspectives. This helps us to better triangulate and discern our own position. Again, I leave this up to the Holy Spirit to do. I am relying on him to do anything that may be of benefit to you as you read this book.

COGNITIVE BIASES

When our paradigms are challenged and stretched, we must consider how our mind processes information. As we go through life, we must make a lot of decisions and judgements. We would like to think that we're capable of taking in and processing all the information we're encountering—in the moment we are experiencing it. However, it would take an excessive amount of time to make the simplest decisions if we considered every possible perspective that would help us to make objective and unbiased ones. We're simply not able to think of every possibility and evaluate it.

To make decisions, our brains (being the powerful "supercomputer" that they are) help to speed things up. They simplify the processing of information and create mental shortcuts

Introduction

called *heuristics*. While these shortcuts help us to make decisions quicker, they often lead to flawed thought processes. These flawed thought processes are called *cognitive biases*.

To combat these flawed thought processes—these cognitive biases, they need to be exposed so that we can become aware of them. We need to familiarize ourselves with their effect on how we think. I have included a chart of 188 cognitive biases in the appendix of this book. The chart is broken up onto four pages, but it can be found in its entirety at the website listed in the image credits.

While there is no way for us to be mindful of all 188 of these cognitive biases in real-time, if we're aware of them and understand how they can weaken our judgment and cause us to make poor decisions, there is a better chance that we can overcome their effect on our thinking. Armed with knowledge and a broadened perspective, we can be better prepared to combat our tendency to hurry through the decision-making process using heuristics and use wisdom instead.

***

Michelangelo wrote in his diary that his mind was a battlefield. If you are making an impact for the Kingdom of God, it's likely that yours is too. The enemy would love for the thinking patterns of church leaders to follow the path of least resistance and go-with-the-flow of mainstream thought without taking time to "demolish arguments and ideas, every high-and-mighty philosophy that pits itself against the knowledge of the *one true* God...taking prisoners of every thought."[1]

Awareness of these cognitive biases which we unconsciously use every day will help us to challenge the heuristics we have created and expand our arsenal of mental weaponry against them. This will help us to think more clearly about how

---

1. 1 Corinthians 10:5 (VOICE)

we'll lead our ministries in these areas. Each of the five commands that are taken from Solomon's soliloquy is applied to church leadership. They will address a cognitive bias that could impair a church leader's judgement.

THE POWER OF STORIES

Gillespie and the Guards

There is a children's book entitled *Gillespie and the Guards* that tells a story about a King that stationed guards at his palace gate. These guards were world-renowned for being the greatest guards that had ever been. They were so great that absolutely nothing could escape their attention. The king was so confident in the ability of these guards that he decided to issue a challenge: if anyone could steal anything from the palace, they would receive a reward.

A young boy decided that he would take the king up on his challenge. One day he entered the palace grounds and, on his way out, tried to pass the guards with a wagon full of rocks. This was no challenge for the well-seasoned guards who quickly stopped him. The boy emptied the wagon of rocks and took his wagon with him. The next day, he tried to take a wagon full of sand past the guards, but to no avail. He again emptied the wagon of sand and proceeded to return home empty-handed with his empty wagon. Repeatedly the boy tried to remove something from the palace, and each time, and without any difficulty, the guards would stop the boy and send him on his way empty-handed with his wagon.

One day the boy appeared before the king and requested to receive his reward. To his astonishment, the king reminded the boy that his guards had successfully thwarted his attempts to steal from the palace. Gillespie answered, "Your majesty the king—they stopped me from stealing the rocks and sand from the palace, but they didn't stop me from stealing the wagons!"

I remember this story from when I was a little boy. That's because we all love stories. When we were children, life came to a standstill when someone opened a storybook and began to bring the words that were written on the page to life (and it didn't hurt if there were pictures to help the imagination along). I've been in church my entire life and have heard more points preached than are on three strands of barbed-wire fence surrounding a ranch in west Texas. Most of them I don't remember, but it's interesting that I can remember more about the points of a message where stories were used to introduce what was to be communicated by the speaker as they unpacked their message.

The reason for this is that stories have staying power in our minds. In her book, *The God-Hungry Imagination*, Sarah Arthur offers a reason why a story has staying power. She writes,

> Story incarnates meaning, embodies content, rather than confronting the hearer's reason with propositional argument. It presents itself in non-threatening ways so that the hearer's defenses are down; it slips past those "watchful dragons" and makes connections that are not easily forgotten.

Everyone is wired for stories. Whether it is toddlers listening to a story book, teenagers watching a movie, or the elderly telling stories from their past to one another—we pay attention when a good story is being told.

This isn't a book whose chapters are full of facts intended to convince you of a premise I'm attempting to make or that tells you *what* to think. I want to first provide you with proofs that will draw you in and begin to get you *to* think. To engage you in the conversation, each of the five lessons will present you with a story that is based on a historical perspective. There will also be references to Biblical stories that will offer you an anchor from God's Word on which to ground the lesson.

By starting with a story, I want to provide you with proof before I try to establish a premise. I need a fighting chance against the heuristics that are pre-loaded into your mind at this point. I hope to disarm any attempt your mind may make to reject the perspective that I am trying to expose you to before it's ever able to be considered. Don't view this as a tactic to combat *your* presently-held thinking patterns on the topic. Instead, I am using story as a tactic to (1) expose and combat the *lack of* thinking that is a result of how strongly cognitive biases cloud our minds from thinking objectively, and (2) to get you clearly thinking about each of these topics as they relate to church leadership.

Watchful Dragons

C.S. Lewis was once asked why it was so hard to feel the way that somebody else told them that they *should* feel about stories related to their Christianity, which included the Passion of Jesus. To this, he responded,

> Supposing that by casting all these things into an imaginary world, stripping them of their stained-glass and Sunday school associations, one could make them for the first time appear in their real potency? Could one not thus steal past those watchful dragons?

Those "watchful dragons" are like the king's guards that stand watch over our minds. Stationed as gatekeepers and tasked with guarding us from being manipulated and from having our currently-held (and maybe deeply-held) beliefs sabotaged are the dragons of distrust and doubt. This is where story will be used

Introduction

like the young boy's wagon. By using stories, the life-giving lessons to be communicated are "stripped of their stained-glass and Sunday school associations" and, without being stopped, allowed to pass by the dragons that are standing on-guard at your mind. As Sarah Arthur puts it,

> Story famously subverts its themes or overall messages by keeping them beneath the surface, which is why the hearer's defenses are down and he or she is more willing to listen. In the most subversive stories, such as parables, the storyteller may even choose to hide or obscure as much or more than he reveals. Subversion allows for truth to sink in slowly over time— **delayed epiphany**. It puts great faith in the hearer's imagination to keep mulling things over long after "The End."

This book is written with this approach at its core. More truth is hidden and obscured than is shown and written. I hope that after reading each chapter that the stories and thoughts will continue to time-release in your mind. As you continue to extrapolate the subverted truths and make connections in your own mind, what you get out of this book will be more beneficial and significant than what I could ever write. While I'll be speaking directly and without subversion at times, I trust that I have waited until the right times to do so.

QUESTIONS AS ANSWERS

I've found in my own life that whenever I'm faced with a problem that spawns a question, I begin looking for answers. I anticipate finding an answer that ends with a period. What I've discovered is that some of the best answers I have received don't end with a period, but end with a question mark. Questions-as-answers cause me to look at the source of my original question deeper.

While I would love to be handed an answer to my question(s) that would provide me with a solution in the short term, it wouldn't help me to become wise in learning *how* to think over the long term. Oftentimes we pray that we might possess the mind of God. It's hard to have that prayer answered if we're always handed an answer without being taught how to think like God thinks.

We typically look to books to provide us with definitive answers for problems that we're currently facing. An author will—like a good television commercial—expose the reader to a problem and then offer solutions chapter-by-chapter to solve the problem they exposed us to. Many books are declarative in nature and lay out pathways of thought or action that the author tells us that we should incorporate into our lives. I want this book to be more inquisitive in nature, leaving you with questions that you'll ask both to yourself and to the Holy Spirit so that the two of you can together determine a pathway of thought or action for your life and leadership.

STRUCTURE

Each chapter in this book begins with a quote that's related to the lesson from Solomon. I encourage you to reread the quote after you finish each chapter and see how it affects you differently than before you read the chapter.

I'll begin the chapter with a historical story. Some of the stories I've carried around in my head for years. They have helped to frame my own thoughts. While I didn't create the stories, I'm so excited to share them with you, and hope that you'll find a depth of meaning in them as I have.

These stories will not only contain a subversive truth, but they'll also illustrate a cognitive bias that has the possibility of clouding your ability to think clearly. The origination of the cognitive bias along with how it works will be unfolded, and you'll see the lesson provided by Solomon begin to surface as we relate it to church leadership.

Each chapter is laced with more stories and insights from books I've read (many of which are in my own personal library) that lend their voice to the conversation. They're not intended to be sources of authority that will tell you the errancy of your thinking or confirm the soundness of your thinking. Their inclusion is meant to help you form a paradigm from which to view the topic and texturize the content. The insertion of my own thoughts and insights are meant to do the same. Many of the thoughts contained here are what I get to share in the classroom to my students who take my classes. For everyone else, I wanted to record them in this book.

Without exception, we'll look to God's Word as the source of all wisdom as he's the giver of it. We'll take a deep dive into the historical aspects of some passages that will supply a biblical framework from which to investigate each topic. The Holy Spirit has a way of illuminating truth from God's Word and making relevant what it says about issues that can have a significant impact on the success (or failure) of the Church which belongs to Jesus.

As leaders appointed by Christ to oversee and shepherd his Church, we must humbly approach our responsibility to steward our leadership well and not allow our thoughts to become the ultimate source of authority for how we'll choose to lead. We must take a seat around the boardroom table and allow the CEO to speak to us from his authoritative Word, directing us in how we're to lead his Church.[1]

---

1. 2 Timothy 3:16

"So above all, guard the affections of your heart, for they affect all that you are. Pay attention to the welfare of your innermost being, for from there flows the wellspring of life."

Proverbs 4:23 (TPT)

ONE

THE OCEAN'S DEEP SECRET:
Guarding Your Heart & the Survivor Bias

> *"Diagoras, who is called the atheist, being at Samothrace, one of his friends showed him several pictures of people who had endured very dangerous storms; 'See,' says he, 'you who deny a providence, how many have been saved by their prayers to the gods.' 'Ay,' says Diagoras, 'I see those who were saved, but where are those painted who were shipwrecked?'"*
>
> —Cicero, *of the Nature of the Gods*

ABRAHAM WALD

If you were part of a bomber crew during World War II, your chances of survival were slim. Members on the crew of a bomber plane were required to complete thirty missions. There was only a twenty-nine percent chance that they would return home safely. A Marine Corps soldier fighting in hand-to-hand combat on the ground stood a better chance of survival than did a crew member of a B-17 bomber aircraft carrying four tons of bombs and one-and-a-half tons of machine gun ammunition. While three to four ground troops were killed for each

Soliloquy № 7

one that was wounded, six bomber crewmen were killed for each one wounded. By the time the war had ended, 12,000 heavy bomber planes had been shot down, killing over 100,000 crewmen. These numbers are staggering, but they could have been a lot worse if not for an unlikely hero by the name of Abraham Wald.

Abraham Wald's heroism was not a result of his being a skilled pilot. He didn't outmaneuver or evade enemy fire from both air and ground attacks. Rather, his heroism came from his ability to solve complex math equations. This would be an unlikely weapon that would lead to several hundred thousand American lives being saved.

Since childhood, Wald had been studying equations and solving the most difficult of math problems. He had emerged as a genius when it came to matters involving probability and statistics. In 1938, Wald chose to move to the United States amid the Nazi threat. Upon arriving, he joined the ranks of an elite team of mathematicians assembled by the federal government. They were known as the Statistical Research Group. His mathematical expertise in statistical analysis would help him to solve one of the war's biggest problems—keeping allied airplanes in the sky so that they could reach their targets and win the war.

The Army Air Force needed to figure out how they could improve the chances of their bombers carrying out their missions and make it safely back home without being shot down by enemy fire. They already knew that the airplanes needed more armor to reinforce the underside of the plane. Figuring out which areas needed the reinforcement most was the problem they were faced with. Naturally, they couldn't add more armor to the entire underside of the airplane. It would never be able to get off the ground because of the additional weight that was added.

Researchers from the Center for Naval Analyses had previously studied the damage that had been done to bombers that were able to return safely from their missions. They took note of where each bullet hole was located. Their findings showed that the bombers had taken fire to the wings, to the center of the plane, and around the tail gunner. The conclusion was that additional reinforcement should be added to the areas where the bullet holes were commonly present.

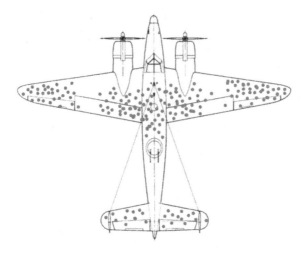

Image collectively charting where bullet holes had penetrated returning B-26 bombers

Instead of confirming the researchers' conclusion, Wald did something extraordinary which would prevent the military from making a terrible mistake. He instantly suggested reinforcing the areas where *no* bullet holes were found. But why did he make this suggestion? Could Wald not see the obvious—that the aircraft were consistently hit in the same areas? Clearly these were the areas that needed to be reinforced with armor.

What wasn't obvious to the researchers was glaringly obvious to Wald. It was evident that all of these bombers had proven that they could receive enemy fire in the same areas and still manage to make it home. It might have seemed like the damaged areas needed the additional reinforcement. However, Wald saw these as the strongest parts of the plane—where they *could* be shot and still return to base. Clearly these planes were parked right in front of them! Wald also pointed out the fact that the researchers were only studying the bombers that had returned safely from their mission—the survivors. The *real* information about which areas of the plane that needed reinforcement was laying somewhere on the bottom of the ocean. Those planes were not around to be inspected.

It seemed to Wald that if a bomber could survive damage to the wings, body, and rear gunner sections, then the undamaged areas of the returning aircraft would undoubtedly be where the armor should be applied. After all, if the bombers that didn't return from their mission had been shot in the same areas that the surviving aircraft had been, he concluded that they, too, would be sitting on the runway.

Logically, what the researchers were hoping to accomplish was to find the weakest areas of the aircraft and then strengthen those areas. What they *actually* ended up doing was focusing their attention on the aircraft that survived and identified the strongest portions of the aircraft. They had completely overlooked the bombers that had been shot in their weakest parts and didn't make it home. The analysts had succumbed to the Survivor bias.

THE SURVIVOR BIAS

In the 1990's, a trio of economists[1] identified a bias that had financial analysts boasting about how some mutual funds were

---

1. In their paper, Elton, Gruber, and Blake eliminated survivorship bias by following the returns on all funds extant at the end of 1976. They showed that other researchers have drawn false conclusions by failing to include the bias in returns on fund performance. Edwin J. Elton, Martin J. Gruber, and Christopher R. Blake "Survivor Bias and Mutual Fund Performance," *The Review of Financial Studies* 9, no. 4 (October 1996): 1097–1120.

The Ocean's Deep Secret: Guarding Your Heart & the Survivor Bias

performing. Mutual funds are made up of successful companies that are generating money *at present*. The funds that have companies that aren't doing well are often merged into other funds to hide the fact that they are losing money. When this happens, a mutual fund can be made to appear profitable when it actually isn't. The "successful" mutual fund was merely compared to other mutual funds that ended up closing because of poor performance. They labeled this the "survivorship bias" or *Survivor bias*.

The Survivor bias happens when we look only at survivors or "successes" and overlook those that aren't. It's easier to examine what has survived than it is to examine what can't be viewed. If we can't inspect the non-survivors, then we naturally give all of our attention to the successful survivors. What's important to success but missing from view is the information possessed by the failures. Without realizing it, we fail to recognize that there's missing information that's very important.

While working on my master's degree, I was enrolled in a course called, "Vision Centered Leadership and Management." One of our required textbooks was a new book that had just been published, entitled *Good to Great: Why Some Companies Make the Leap-and Others Don't* by Jim Collins. The book was a study of several elite companies that made the transition from being just a long-term "good" company to becoming a long-term "great" company. In order to be identified as a great company, it had to have fifteen years of stable returns, followed by fifteen years of returns that beat the general Stock Market by an average of seven times. Out of the 1,435 companies that Collins studied, only eleven were identified as "great."

Collins had conducted a five-year study of those eleven companies. He was looking for shared characteristics that existed in all the companies which might account for their success. Identified were seven clearly defined characteristics that these successful companies had in common. These characteristics were compared with other companies in the same industry and of similar size but which had failed to become great.

Then, Collins examined the CEO's of these successful companies, and he identified the common characteristics that they shared with one another.

In essence, what Collins did was the same thing that the researchers had done with the returning bombers. He examined successful companies that met specific criteria and found the similarities that they shared. Collins took it one step further and identified the similarities of the CEO's who piloted these companies. The reader of his book was left with the impression that, in order to become successful, he or she needed to possess the same characteristics as the ones Collins identified. So, to become a successful leader, you'd need to cultivate into your own leadership the same characteristics that leaders of these successful companies possessed.

Our professor wanted us to notice these characteristics and integrate them into our positions of leadership in the church. The idea was that if we were to do what these successful companies and their CEO's did, we, too, could be successful in our leadership and so would the churches and ministries that we would be leading.

Collins failed, however, to also examine the unsuccessful companies and their leaders. What were the areas of weaknesses that kept them from becoming successful? In his book *Standard Deviations*, Gary Smith noted that Collins had fallen for the Survivor bias. From 2001-2012 (the ten-year period after *Good to Great* was published), Smith continued watching the same eleven companies that Collins had identified as being great. He discovered that, during that subsequent ten-year period, six of the eleven "great" companies had performed worse than the overall Stock Market. Had Collins extended his study out for another ten years, those same "great" companies he originally identified wouldn't have made the cut. They would have been listed among the 1,435 companies that were not so great.

Failure

It's a mistake to try to predict what will make us successful by looking *only* at successful people or organizations and identifying their similarities. The people or organizations that have failed must also be considered. We need to find out what made them *un*successful. The only way to counteract the Survivor bias is to examine both the successful and the unsuccessful. Failure provides us with equally important information about what we need to guard against so that we can avoid failure. The problem is that those organizations and leaders who fail have valuable information to teach us, but they aren't readily available to us so that we can learn from them.

Church leaders succumb to the Survivor bias as well. Successful pastors and churches who survive the challenges that they are presented with are the ones we look to for the clues we think will lead us to success in our own leadership and ministries. We want to know what it takes to grow numerically as they have. We want to know how to engage culture and be accepted by society as they have. We want to know what successful pastors who have emerged from adversity and struggles did to become great leaders of their churches.

These "successful" leaders are the ones who are invited to be our conference speakers. They're the ones who write the books that we want to read and whose podcasts and videos we want to listen to and watch. They talk about their journey and what they did along the way that made them successful. We inspect every element of their ministry or leadership and begin to emulate their worship styles, preaching styles, ministry environments, and personal or leadership practices. We attribute their success to what they are currently doing or have previously done in order to get them where they are now. We believe that by incorporating these elements into our own church or leadership it will cause us to become successful too.

Soliloquy № 7

But have you ever seen a conference advertised where all the speakers were *unsuccessful* in their leadership or ministry? That would be quite the opposite of what we're used to seeing promoted! I can imagine such relevant topics such as:

- "How to Have a Moral Failure"
- "Five Keys to Get Your Church Attendance to Numerically Plateau or Decline"
- "The Secret to Becoming Missionally Ineffective Without Anyone Noticing"
- "Developing a Strategic Plan to Build Your Own Empire Instead of God's Kingdom"

I don't think that anyone would attend a conference like this because of how biased we have become to survivorship. We live in a "study-the-successful" culture. Our belief is that if we do the things that successful churches, ministries, and leaders do, we won't become a failure; we, too, will become successful. However, the most important information about becoming successful is gathered by looking at the leaders and churches or ministries that ended up failing and discovering what made them fail.

Failure teaches us about what *not* to do or what we should avoid. If we neglect looking for that information, the result is a runway full of successful churches and leaders who have "made it." These successful churches, ministries, and leaders provide us only with information about their areas of strength. They never seem to reveal very much about the weaknesses that they must constantly reinforce that could cause them to fail. That information is hidden from sight and is not factored into what has made them a success. Author, Alicia Britt Chole once said that "failure is a powerful teacher if we would only let her speak." We're more intent on listening to what success has to say than we are to failure.

Success

In his book, *Antifragile: Things That Gain from Disorder*, Nassim Nicholas Taleb wrote about how he had searched history for heroes who became heroes for what they did *not* do. He said that he couldn't easily find any because it's hard to observe non-action. Taleb further stated that in our professionalized society it's easier to sell "Look what I did" than it is "Look what I avoided." *Our culture rewards performance and not avoidance.* This mentality finds its way into our churches, ministries, and leadership practices.

We all want to be "heroes" in the Kingdom of God. Perhaps we feel that to become one, we have to do things that separate us from the ordinary. When we look at our church-world heroes, the Survivor bias causes us to focus on the performance measures of those whom we deem as successful without examining their avoidance measures. Church and ministry leaders must take the time to probe the leaders, churches, and ministries whom we view as successful and find the areas where these have *avoided* failure. We must also take time to probe those leaders, churches, and ministries that are unsuccessful for areas that they have *experienced* failure.

For example, we could look at churches that are growing numerically and observe that they are all operating multi-site campuses, writing their own worship songs, and have lead pastors that are preaching in flip-flops. If every church were to do these things, would they be guaranteed numerical growth in their own churches as well? Before launching a multi-site strategy of our own, writing our own worship songs, or attempting to adopt the clothing styles of these leaders, it would be wise for us to examine what those successful churches, ministries, and leaders have also *avoided* and what unsuccessful ones didn't. There are churches that have copied the behaviors of successful churches and ministers as mentioned above (and more) only to experience failure.

Soliloquy № 7

Perhaps the entire leadership staff of a successful church has avoided allowing their private devotional lives to be overrun by the daily demands of doing ministry. Maybe they have avoided the temptation to preach a socially acceptable gospel and are committed to preaching a gospel that may offend the "flesh" but will liberate the spirit. It could be that the leadership of unsuccessful churches began depending on their own strengths, talents, and techniques for church growth rather than on God's Spirit to draw people to repentance and grow his Church. Success in God's Kingdom is achieved not only by what we do but also by what we do *not* do.

It's impossible to predict what will make us successful if we don't also consider what would cause us to become unsuccessful. Imagine if Peter were asked, "How do you successfully walk on water?" His reply might be, "Do *not* take your eyes off of Jesus." There wasn't anything he could do in order to walk on water. The only way he could walk on water was to *not* do something. When we look only at success, there are far too many factors to consider that may contribute to it. We must also look at failure for factors that could keep us from it.

What lies at the heart of the matter is how we define success.

DEFINING SUCCESS

The definition of success plagued me during the first ten years of my ministry. I couldn't seem to pinpoint what constituted a "win" in my leadership and in my ministry. Was success numerical growth? No. Numerical growth is a by-product of success. Was success financial solvency? No. That's another by-product of success. Was it having the admiration of my leadership, congregation, and denomination for what I was attempting to do for God? That, too, is another by-product.

It's difficult to establish a clear indicator of success that we can all agree on because God has each of us in different places, under differing circumstances, and with tasks that differ from one another according to his timing, will, and purposes. If success is a number, which number is it, and is it the same number for everyone? If it's a ratio or percentage, what's the number? Who established it, and where did they get their authority to do so? My dad once told me that success in God's Kingdom was to be obedient and dedicated to what God has called *you* to do. "Well done, good (obedient) and faithful (dedicated) servant."[1]

Paul & The Philippian Rivals

Recently, on a Sunday morning, my pastor started preaching through the book of Philippians. The text that he covered included a portion of scripture where Paul was talking about a group of Christian believers in the church at Philippi who were not preaching the gospel with pure motives. Towards the beginning of his letter Paul wrote,

> Some indeed preach Christ from envy and rivalry, but others from good will. The later do it out of love, knowing that I am put here for the defense of the gospel. The former proclaim Christ out of selfish ambition, not sincerely but thinking to afflict me in my imprisonment.[2]

Now this may seem an unusual passage of scripture to include here as I'm writing about success in ministry. It appears to have nothing to do with the topic of defining success.

As my pastor preached, I became curious about who these rivals were that were preaching the gospel out of selfish ambition and using the gospel as a platform to afflict Paul in his

---

1. Matthew 25:21 (NLT)
2. Philippians 1:15-17

imprisonment. So, later during that week, I went to the library at the university where I teach and began looking deeper into this passage. I discovered a theologian by the name of Robert Jewett who had written an article entitled, "Conflicting Movements in the Early Church as Reflected in Philippians" for the journal, *Novum Testamentum*. In it, Jewett suggested a possible motive for why these Christian brothers were acting the way they were (albeit wrongly) towards Paul.

Jewett indicated that the mission strategy of some of the believers in the church at Philippi included the preaching of a "gospel of success." They attempted to prove their claims of the power of God by overcoming all opposition that came against them. With this in mind, if Paul was unable to throw off his prison chains, these individuals saw him as putting the Christian message in jeopardy. Paul's definition of success and the definition of those who preached a gospel out of selfish ambition was totally different. To these rivals, Paul's imprisonment was taken as a sign of weakness and that he really didn't know about the power of Christ.

The fact that Paul was inside the prison and not outside of it would have caused them to view Paul as their rival, and they were distancing themselves from him because of his failure to be successful (according to their theology and what they were preaching). For Paul to be seen as successful (according to their strategy) he would have either had to not go to prison or not have been in prison very long because operating within the power of Christ meant having success.

Unfortunately, there are churches, ministries, and leaders who have—either consciously or unconsciously—prescribed to a gospel of success as some in the church of Philippi had. Could it be that there are some who lead and operate their ministries out of a spirit of envy and rivalry in today's church culture? The inferiority complex that some church and ministry leaders possess can cause them to become envious of other churches, ministries, and leaders whom they define as successful. The leadership of God's Church—designed to be one body with many parts and commissioned to make disciples—become rivals of one another. It's as if each wants to be viewed by others as more successful than their "competitors."

We've become so preoccupied with looking at all the areas where successful ministry leaders have been attacked but emerged victorious—a gospel of success. By doing so, what we've overlooked are the vital areas that haven't brought down these ministries and leaders when they were attacked, and how they have strategically reinforced those areas.

The individuals in the Philippian church would have preferred for Paul to reinforce the non-vital areas (such as taking measures to *not* end up in prison) so that enemy fire would not "penetrate his wings." This would have given the *appearance* of a demonstration of the power of God. To these Philippian rivals, it would have shown others that God would make one successful by what his power could keep believers *from*. God, however, wanted to demonstrate the real power that's available to believers, showing that success is achieved by relying on his power to bring them *through*.

Paul chose to reinforce the vital areas of his life so that both he and others might place greater trust in God's powerful abilities. After witnessing what God's power can do in the midst of being attacked by the enemy, a *real* demonstration of the power of God that will make one successful can be observed. God has the ability to sustain believers as they go through extreme trials without the enemy being victorious over God's will for their lives.

Because of Paul's prison sentence, you and I (as well as countless other believers) have been blessed to read the sentences of his prison epistles found in Ephesians, Philippians, Colossians, and Philemon. These letters have been used to help church and ministry leaders reinforce vital areas of our lives where the enemy targets us in an attempt to render the will of God ineffective.

Soliloquy № 7

The definition of success is actually not determined by how successful we are as defined by others. It's determined by *not* being unsuccessful in what God has defined as success for us. Paul might not have been successful in evading jail time, but he was successful in patiently enduring suffering for the cause of Christ. These Philippian rivals had measured success in terms of what the power of the Christian message could keep them from rather than what it could bring them through.

We should guard and reinforce personal discipleship, prayer, fasting, holy living, faith, and the power of God's Word applied to our lives. Taleb warned his readers not to listen to those who give you positive advice and *only* positive advice. Those who are truly successful also glean from the negative.

The Lampstand: Shedding Some Light on What Makes Us Successful

The second and third chapters of Revelation are written to the churches of the seven most populous, wealthy, and influential areas in the province of Asia. Most of these churches would have been considered successful according to our metrics today. They had lots of people, money, and influence (except perhaps for the church in Smyrna who was experiencing tribulation and poverty, yet Jesus said it was rich). It's through these seven churches that John's letter would find its way to other churches in the area as these seven were all located on a major circular road that connected them to one another.

When Jesus addressed these churches, he pointed out what made them so great (except for Laodicea that fit the definition of success but was a failure). By the way, they didn't all have the same areas of strength. Their strengths were commended according to the context that they were in. He identified where they'd been attacked but had proven to be strong. Jesus also pointed out their areas of weakness and what would bring them down if they didn't guard those areas.

Unlike their strengths which varied according to context, the weaknesses he identified in each of them would have caused *any* of them to be unsuccessful. He went further and told them what they needed to do to correct their mistakes. It was as if Jesus told them that if they wanted to be a survivor, they had to reinforce where they were most vulnerable. Jesus not only identified what made these churches great (which was not their numbers, finances, or influence), but he also identified what would bring them down.

John, the Apostle who wrote the book of Revelation, was told that these churches were each symbolized by a golden lampstand:

> Then I turned to see the voice that was speaking to me, and on turning I saw seven golden lampstands...[which] are the seven churches.[1]

In order to better understand what Christ was saying to the seven churches as he spoke through John, we need to examine the lampstand a little closer. God first gave Moses instructions for building the lampstand.[2] It was to be placed inside the tabernacle on the south side across from the Table of Showbread which was positioned on the north side of the tabernacle.[3]

Additionally, the lampstand was to shine the light forward.[4] If the lampstand was situated across from the Table of Showbread and positioned so that the light shined forward, then the lampstand's main function was to shine light on the bread.

---

1. Revelation 1:12, 20
2. Exodus 25:31-40
3. Exodus 26:35; 40:24
4. Exodus 25:37

Soliloquy № 7

While everything in the interior of the tabernacle would be touched by and be illuminated by the light of the lampstand, the light was to be directed towards the bread.

Metaphorically speaking, if Jesus is the Bread of Life[1] and the Church is the lampstand,[2] then the Church exists to illuminate Jesus so that he can be seen. If our churches, ministries, and their leaders are to be successful in the eyes of God, then their primary function is to stay full of oil with their wicks trimmed and pointed in the right direction. *This* is success!

Further substantiating this as *the* success metric is the fact that no measurements were given to Moses for how big to build the lampstand (interestingly, there are no measurements given for the bronze laver either). Given this fact, it would seem to signify that church size doesn't matter and is not a valid measurement of success. What *does* matter is that whatever size a church or ministry may be, its function is to shine the light on Jesus and make him known. A small lamp full of oil with wicks trimmed and pointing in the right direction fulfills more of its intended function than does a big lamp with very little or no oil, untrimmed wicks, and pointing in the wrong direction.

Catherine Aird wrote a line in her book, *His Burial Too,* that has become a popular maxim: "If…you can't be a good example, then you'll just have to be a horrible warning." Small churches and ministries with meager budgets and unknown leaders who are shining the light on Jesus serve as better examples of what God wants his Church to be. They are more successful than large churches and ministries with bountiful budgets and well-known leaders who don't function the way God intended for his Church to function. These should be to us horrible warnings of failure if we're looking to Christ for what determines success rather than looking to other churches, ministries, and their

---

1. John 6:35
2. Revelation 1:12, 20

leaders to define success for us. "For *where two or three* gather together as my followers, I am there among them."[1]

Zacchaeus & the Rich Ruler

An extremely rich ruler had certain characteristics of someone who would be considered successful in God's Kingdom.[2] The notes in the *Fire Bible* state that up until this time, the disciples likely held the same view as most Jews of that day—that riches were usually a sign of God's favor and approval. The ruler had not committed adultery, had not murdered, had not stolen, had not born false witness, and had honored his father and mother. It can be assumed, however, that there were many Jews who had kept these commands since they were young as well, but they were *not* rich and successful. Also, there were Jews who were rich and successful but hadn't kept these commands.

One such person was Zacchaeus. Just a few verses after the story of the rich ruler, Luke tells us that Zacchaeus was also extremely wealthy.[3] From what I know about Zacchaeus, he was a sinner who had not kept the commands like the ruler had even though he was also a Jew. If success in God's Kingdom had been determined by material wealth according to the views held at that time, it was an unreliable indicator. If we established wealth as the determining factor of success, then we could put both Zacchaeus and the ruler on the runway. We could then begin to look for similarities between these two men.

Both were law-abiding men. The ruler lived his life according to the law of God, and Zacchaeus lived his according to the law of the land that permitted him to collect taxes. From

---

1. Matthew 18:20 (NLT)
2. Luke 18:18-23
3. Luke 19:1-9

this, we could draw a conclusion that if you live your life according to the law, you would become wealthy which would indicate your success in achieving God's favor and approval.

But, if success were to be measured by obedience to God — by possessing the heart of Christ and not merely keeping the law of God, then Zacchaeus would be the only one on the runway. The ruler identified himself with God's law, but it didn't produce the heart of Christ within him. Because of this, he wasn't willing to part with his riches and meet the needs of the poor around him. Zacchaeus, however, identified with the heart of Christ (even though he hadn't kept the law of God) which resulted in his being willing to give half of his wealth to the poor. The ruler attempted to become successful through *addition* — trying to do what was Godly in order to find eternal life; Zacchaeus would become successful by *subtraction* — taking away what wasn't Godly in order to find eternal life.

This reminds me of the prayer that Jabez prayed: "Oh that you would bless me and enlarge my border"[1] — add to what I have and give me more! We pray this prayer for our personal lives and for our ministries, wanting God to give us more and increase our success. But when you think of God as being the potter and us, the clay, the way he enlarges our borders so that we have the ability to possess more is by reaching his hand inside of our lives or ministries and removing more of the clay inside. Enlarged borders are achieved through subtraction, not addition.

Notice that Jesus never asked Zacchaeus to give half his wealth to the poor. Zacchaeus measured his life in comparison with the heart of Jesus, but the ruler measured his life in comparison with the law. According to these two men, if you want to be successful in God's Kingdom, you may or may not have kept his laws from childhood, but you absolutely can't be successful if you don't have God's heart. And success will not be

---

1. 1 Chronicles 4:10

established by quantifiable measures such as attendance numbers, offering size, or denominational influence.

THE "TAKE-AWAY"

There is a story about Michelangelo who was once asked by the Pope about his secret to being a successful sculptor. The Pope was curious as to how Michelangelo had carved the statue of David, which is considered to be the masterpiece of all masterpieces. Michelangelo's answer was: "It's simple. I just remove everything that is not David."

Becoming a church or ministry leader that is God's masterpiece is more about subtraction than it is addition. We must look at ourselves and remove everything that is not Jesus. We must become knowledgeable about what will keep us from being successful. This would include examining the areas of other ministers and ministries where they have experienced failure. If we will do this, we won't have to run around looking at survivors and try to find what made them successful.

Taleb calls this *subtractive epistemology*. When you remove what is wrong, you can discover what is right. He says that we know a lot more about what is wrong than about what is right. What we believe will make us successful today might turn out to be wrong tomorrow, but what we know will cause us to be unsuccessful can *never* turn out to be right.

According to Taleb, there is a theological tradition, particularly in the Eastern Orthodox Church, called *via negativa*—the "negative way"—that focuses on negative description. He states, "It doesn't try to express what God is. It just lists what God is *not* and proceeds by the process of elimination." The "negative way" of becoming a successful church or ministry leader is to identify what a successful leader is *not* (based on what we know from God's Word and from those who have

Soliloquy № 7

been unsuccessful) and then work with obedience and dedication toward becoming faithful to what God has called us to do.

Admonishment #1: Above all, guard the affections of your heart. Reinforce the areas of your life that are vital and will bring you down if not guarded.

Questions:

- What areas of your church, ministry, or life do *you* need to guard and reinforce so that you can be successful?
- What are other churches and ministries guarding and reinforcing?
- What do leaders whom you view as successful guard against and reinforce in their lives?
- What areas did unsuccessful churches, ministries, or leaders *not* guard that led to their downfall?
- Are there any areas of your life or ministry that are in need of subtraction in order to look more like the success that God wants you to become?

"Avoid dishonest speech and pretentious words. Be free from using perverse words no matter what!"

Proverbs 4:24 (TPT)

Two

FASHION STATEMENTS:
Avoiding Deceitful Communication & Enclothed Cognition

"Good clothes open all doors."

—Thomas Fuller, *Gnomologia*

CLOTHING LAYER #1:
BASE LAYER

FEATHERS

One of the legendary symbols of Native American culture is the feather. For Native American tribes, feathers have served as a symbol of wisdom, peace, and power (among other things). The meaning of a feather depended on which type of bird that the feather came from. Birds were revered as messengers and spirit guides that would appear at different times during the lifetime of a tribal member. They believed that birds would bring wisdom and protection, and that they would bestow these things upon people with a gift of one of their feathers.

Native Americans were Animists. This meant that they held the belief that everything in the world possessed a soul or a spirit. When they had received a feather from a bird, they believed it had been sent to them. They saw the feather as a vessel that transferred all of the energies of the bird to one thought worthy enough to deserve the honor. The feather was viewed as a gift that bore a spiritual purpose.

For the Native American, everything was associated with a purpose. The feathers of different birds came in various colors which the Native American referred to as "signs." Even in our own culture today, colors influence how we think, feel, and act. For the Native American, receiving good signs such as these meant having good connections with the Spirit.

Orange feathers depicted physical love, creativity, energy, optimism, and success. Pink ones denoted romance, friendship, compassion, empathy, kindness, and inspiration. If a feather were red, this signified passion, courage, and good fortune. Feathers that were blue embodied communication, peace,

Clothing Layer #1: BASE LAYER

knowledge, and spiritual protection. It was believed that purple ones represented higher thought and higher spirituality. Black feathers represented growth, protection, and the ending of something. White ones were a symbol of peace, purification, and faith. And when the feather had a shimmering sheen, it was said to possess high mystical insight.

Star Feathers

There is a Native American legend from the Cherokee tribe about a warrior who journeyed east and came upon a "white man's" settlement. As he had roamed around the settlement, he saw—for the very first time—a peacock. The young warrior was so taken with the beauty of the long, colorful feathers that he traded some of his most valuable possessions to acquire just a few of them. When he had returned to his own land, he took the feathers to the mountains and put them in an old beaver lodge that was hidden underneath a river bank. There, the warrior began to make for himself a headdress out of the peacock feathers. He put some of the longer ones in the front which trailed out behind him and some of the shorter ones at the sides.

At the next tribal dance, he wore the headdress he'd made and told everyone that he had journeyed to the sky and acquired these special "star feathers." As the tribe looked at these star feathers, the warrior began to make a long speech which he claimed he'd received from the star spirits to deliver to his people. The people of the tribe had never seen such beautiful feathers. They were so different from the ones with which they were acquainted. There could be no doubt that he had indeed been up to the sky and received this message from the spirits.

To the tribe, this warrior had become a great prophet. He would hide himself in the beaver lodge until there was a night gathering for a dance or a council. Then, he would appear and give another prophecy which he claimed to have received from

Soliloquy № 7

the sky. Afterwards, he would leave and pretend to ascend into the sky. After many times of doing this, the medicine men of the village revered him, and he became powerful and famous. Meanwhile, another of the Cherokee braves journeyed to one of the "white man's" settlements where he, too, encountered a beautiful peacock. After seeing the same beautiful feathers that the bird displayed, he knew that the warrior-prophet was a fraud.

When the tribal dance had taken place the next night, the prophet who claimed to have come down from the sky with a new message from the stars delivered his prophecy. The people intently listened and vowed to do everything that the prophet had instructed. After delivering the message, he told the people that he must return to the sky and he slipped into the darkness. Knowing that this prophet was a fake, the brave (who had recently returned) and a few of his friends followed him into the darkness and watched him as he headed to the river and dove underneath the water. They waited for him to resurface, but he never did.

The young braves returned to the tribe and told them of what they had discovered. When the sun had risen the next day, a party of scouts was appointed by the tribal elders and sent to the river to investigate. After searching, they discovered the beaver lodge under the bank of the river. One of the young men dove underneath the water and came up into the beaver lodge where he found the prophet sitting with the peacock feather headdress by his side.

This young Cherokee warrior had not been gifted with the shimmery feathers by a peacock. Neither was he given the high mystical insight they symbolized in the exchange. However, when this young warrior wore the feathers, those who understood the symbolism of shimmery feathers and saw him wearing them believed that he'd been given the gift of insight. As it turned out, wearing those feathers had an equally powerful effect on the young warrior when he put on the headdress he'd made. Knowing for himself what they symbolized,

Clothing Layer #1: BASE LAYER

these feathers gave him the confidence to act as one who *had* been given high mystical insight. They caused him to think of himself as one who was worthy of being given messages from the sky spirits when he wore them.

ENCLOTHED COGNITION

Inevitably, we all tend to make initial judgments about someone else or something else in comparison with other people or things. Then, we respond according to the bias that we've subsequently formed. One of the first things we observe about another person is their clothing.[1] (Read the footnote below regarding the first seven things we notice about someone when we see them and notice that *appearance* is the only factor in the list that includes the significant element of clothing which we have choice and control over.)

In his book, *Rise of the Morning Star*, A.J. Darkholme observed,

> It's amazing how just dressing differently can affect your influence; dress like a beggar and your assumed poverty gains you looks of contempt; dress in gold-lined robes and people are more willing to accommodate you; sport armour and you look strong, dutiful, and prepared.

We form a bias based on observations we've made about the world around us. Then, we create stereotypes about people without actually knowing them. It's a kind of social *heuristic* or

---

1. When we encounter another human being, we notice the following about them in this order: (1) skin color, (2) gender, (3) age, (4) bearing – this includes height, head movement and body language, (5) appearance, which includes the (up to) 90% of their person covered in clothing, (6) direct eye contact, and (7) speech.

mental shortcut we make that helps us to try to quickly make sense of our surroundings.

While this is occurring inside the mind of someone who's observing what we're wearing, this same process has already taken place inside our own mind towards the other person. But before we ever stepped foot outside of our home and became visible to others, we made a conscious decision to select the clothing we would wear. All clothing styles (or the way we wear that clothing) have some type of meaning attached to them (e.g., a suit, athletic wear, trendy clothes).

Without asking for our permission, the style or type of clothing that we choose to wear associates us (knowingly or unknowingly) with the stereotype of others who wear the same style or type of clothing. When we put on those clothes, we're affected by the ascribed meaning that's associated with the type or style of that clothing. We unconsciously embody the properties and meanings of our clothes and begin to think, act, and behave according to those attributes. Our clothing sends messages to us before we use them to say something about ourselves to others. The messages our clothes convey to us affect the way we think and act. So, before our clothes say something *about* us, they are saying something *to* us.

Why Doctors Wear White Lab Coats

Researchers[1] have discovered that the physical act of wearing clothes having symbolic meaning prescribed to them causes us to alter our attitudes, behaviors, moods, self-evaluations, personalities, confidence, and interactions with others. All of these are in congruence with the behaviors, attitudes, moods,

---

1. Hajo Adam and Adam D. Galinsky, "Enclothed Cognition," *Journal of Experimental Social Psychology*, vol. 48, no. 4 (July 2012): 918–925.

etc. associated with that clothing. These researchers—psychologists at Northwestern University—coined the term *Enclothed Cognition* after their research discovered the effect that clothing has on us. They published a study demonstrating that clothes do in fact have an effect on the wearer and influence their psychological processes.

The researchers took a lab coat (that has historically been associated with the attitude and behavior of attentiveness and carefulness which scientists who wear them typically exude) and used it in three different experiments. In their first experiment, one-half of the test subjects were given a lab coat and instructed to wear it. They were then administered a Stroop test.[1] Those who physically wore the lab coat while performing the test made half as many errors on the test compared to those who took the Stroop test but were not given a lab coat to wear while being tested.

In their second and third experiments, the researchers gave two groups white coats to wear but told one of the groups that the white coats were doctors' lab coats. The other group was told that they were painters' smocks. A third group was placed in a room that had a white coat lying on a desk near them and were told it was a doctors' lab coat. All three groups were then told to write about what images came to mind when they thought of the meaning of the coat. Next, the researchers had all three groups look at photos that were placed together and asked them to identify minor differences in the photos (which were difficult to find). Those who wore what they thought were painters' smocks found the fewest differences between the pictures. The group that merely *thought* about what they were told was a doctor's lab coat but didn't wear it found more of the

---

[1]. The Stroop Test has the test taker read the name of a color that is printed in a different color than the word. Then, the test-taker is to say the color of ink that the word is printed in rather than the color of the word.

differences. But, those who *wore* what they were told were doctors' lab coats found the most differences between the pictures.

The research concluded that the influence of clothes on the wearer depends on both the symbolic meaning of the clothing *and also the wearing of the clothing*. The astounding thing the researcher's discovered was that when we wear clothes that have some meaning woven into the fabric, we're unconsciously being influenced and adjusting our attitude to behave according to the symbolism of the clothing we're wearing. This takes place before someone else has ever looked at us and what we're wearing.

This effect is not limited to trade-related uniform clothing such as doctor's coats or chef's toques. *Vogue Magazine* asked a few women in a variety of careers about the clothing they wore to work to bring out their best. Some of the women that were interviewed indicated it was a great pair of high heel shoes that created a sense of power for them. Others noted a correlation between certain name brands and the level of confidence they felt as a result of wearing them. None of them talked about what their clothing or name brands did for others, but rather what it did for themselves.

On a personal note, I grew up in the home of a small-church pastor where money *was* an object. When I received hand-me-down name brand clothing from my rich cousin who was a little older than I was, the little tag on the inside of the article of clothing that had the name brand on it might as well have been the cape of a superhero. It had some kind of transformational power on my confidence when I wore those name-brand clothes to school.

Researchers[1] have also uncovered some interesting findings on how various types of clothing can affect the wearer.

---

1. Michael L. Slepian, Simon N. Ferber, Joshua M. Gold, and Abraham M. Rutchick, "The Cognitive Consequences of Formal Clothing," *Social Psychological and Personality Science* 6, no. 6 (2015): 661–68.

They have discovered that wearing a suit makes men feel more confident because of the symbolism of authority, success, and power associated with them. Wearing a suit has been found to cause the wearer to think more broadly and holistically rather than thinking narrowly and getting caught up in straining at the details.

Suits also proved to engage the wearer in abstract processing rather than mere concrete processing. This is beneficial when it comes to how negative information is received. "If you get a stinging piece of critical feedback at work, if you think about it with a concrete processing style, it's more likely to negatively impact your self-esteem," says Michael Slepian, professor of management at Columbia Business School. Interestingly, it has been found that by merely wearing a suit the hormones needed to display dominance can actually increase.[1]

On the other hand, some studies have found that wearing a suit can make the wearer less open, as well as finding it more difficult to relax. When someone puts on casual clothing, however, it has been found to help the wearer be friendlier and more creative.[2] Meanwhile, uniforms (including the liturgical vestments still worn by some in ministry) cause those wearing them to become more aware of their roles and duties associated with them.

There are always tradeoffs when it comes to anything that involves a choice. It's an undisputed fact that people make their initial judgments about us based upon our appearance. We can't control the outcome of other people's judgements. Will

---

1. Michael W. Kraus and Wendy Berry Mendes, "Sartorial Symbols of Social Class Elicit Class-Consistent Behavioral and Physiological Responses: A Dyadic Approach," *Journal of Experimental Psychology: General* 143, no. 6 (2014): 2330–40.

2. Katherine A. Karl, Leda Mcintyre Hall, and Joy V. Peluchette, "City Employee Perceptions of the Impact of Dress and Appearance," *Public Personnel Management* 42, no. 3 (August 16, 2013): 452–70.

Soliloquy № 7

people judge ministers as being relatable and friendly, or will they judge us as not taking our responsibilities seriously? The deeper question we're addressing is how the clothing choices of a church leader affect our *own* attitudes and behaviors as a result of enclothed cognition.

Clothing does in fact seem to possess a powerful influence over the psyche of the wearer. It has been shown to affect people's perceived social status and political views.[1] One particular facet of the influence clothing has on the wearer is that of how clothing can affect our behavior and attitude. An example of this was demonstrated in a study[2] where women were given a handbag to carry made by the designer company, Prada. When carrying the Prada handbag, these women reported that they noticed a boost in how they perceived their social status. This attitude was reflected by their demonstration of more selfish behaviors. When compared to a second group of women in the study who were given a non-luxury handbag to carry, those who carried the Prada handbag were less likely to make charitable contributions unless the opportunity to give would increase their reputation among others. In this case, they contributed more generously than did those given a non-luxury handbag to carry. The researches also discovered that those carrying the luxury handbag exercised more self-control than did those who carried the non-luxury one.

These findings demonstrate that when we dress for whatever role we intend to portray, we start to live in accordance with that role. Our attitudes and behaviors change. To take this

---

1. Yajin Wang and Deborah Roedder John, "Louis Vuitton and Conservatism: How Luxury Consumption Influences Political Attitudes," Thesis. Marketing Department, Carlson School of Management, University of Minnesota, 2015. *Louis Vuitton and Conservatism: How Luxury Consumption Influences Political Attitudes*. Institute for Brands and Brand Relationships, May 27, 2015.

2. Ibid

Clothing Layer #1: BASE LAYER

a step further, what we wear not only affects our own attitudes and behaviors, but it has the potential to affect others' attitudes and behaviors as well. When people base their clothing choices on what others are wearing, it has been found that the mere act of copying the style of someone who's intelligence, power, personality, or influence we admire will cause the imitator to feel infused with the same qualities as the one who's style of dress they are attempting to imitate.[1]

But clothing is an inanimate, mindless, and dependent object! It inherently possesses no power, doesn't exercise its will over the wearer, and doesn't define the meaning of itself. Clothing doesn't come to us by itself in varying degrees of beauty. It doesn't categorize itself in a hierarchy or ascribe a tier of value to itself. All of these things are ascribed to clothing either by the clothing's creator, the wearer, or the observer. If we could only find a pair of glasses like John Nada did, the central character in the movie *They Live*. The glasses he found revealed the hidden reality of subliminal messages hidden all around him. It would be more interesting if we could find a pair of glasses that enabled us to see what other people are unconsciously (or consciously) communicating about themselves through their clothing.

In Joseph Roach's book entitled *It* (which has been described as a consumer's guide to iconic celebrity and ageless glamour), he writes,

> Perhaps part of the uncanny allure of fashionable clothing resides in the paradoxical impact of its expressiveness: the act of covering up with mere dead matter—cloth, fur, leather, or even metal when it is ingeniously shaped to the

---

1. Adam Sicinski, "How to Model Successful People and Develop the Mindset of a High Achiever." IQ Matrix Blog, December 10, 2018.

Soliloquy № 7

purpose—appears to reveal something magical about the life inside.

Clothing not only unconsciously *reveals* something about the life of the person inside of them, but it also unconsciously *affects* the life of the person inside of them. In this way, clothing becomes a means of communication—much like words or symbols. Just as words and symbols have no meaning unless it's ascribed to them by people, clothing is a type of language.

THE LANGUAGE OF CLOTHING

Closely related to the idea that clothing can be used as a vehicle of communication like language is the *ideogram*. The *Merriam-Webster Dictionary* describes ideograms as "pictures or symbols that represent not the object being pictured but some thing or idea that the object pictured is supposed to suggest." The Chinese language is written using ideograms to express words. The words are the visual representations of the ideas each ideogram is expressing. For example, the Chinese word for "sweet" is a combination of the mouth and a 'sweet' thing in it.

gān *(sweet)*

Conveying an idea verbally requires us to string many words together to get a message across to the listener. Both the speaker and the listener must also know the meaning of each word for the message to be conveyed and received accurately. The saying, "A picture says a thousand words" accurately depicts the idea of ideogrammatic language. An idea or thought that might take many spoken words to convey its meaning is put into a picture that speaks the idea, thought, or concept visually without a word being spoken.

It would seem that all clothing has the ability to convey many words as society imputes meaning into them. The clothes we choose to wear become an ideogrammatic language that communicates messages both *to* us and *about* us. Clothing has been programmed with words that describe feelings, emotions, and thoughts. What feelings, thoughts, or emotions come to your mind about someone who is wearing a black leather vest with a motorcycle gang patch on the back? How about a military uniform? What about a T-shirt displaying the name of a popular music band?

After Adam and Eve disobeyed God's command to not eat of the Tree of Knowledge of Good and Evil, Genesis 3:7 states, "At that moment their eyes were opened, and they suddenly felt shame at their nakedness. So, they sewed fig leaves together to cover themselves." It appears clothing became the first material object ever produced by human hands that served as a physical manifestation of the inner creativity and ingenuity of the human mind. They would be the first clothes to embody the expression of a feeling that had given meaning to their clothing.

Adam and Eve felt *shame*, and the clothing they made expressed the shame they felt as they covered their nakedness with leaves. Their clothing ideographically said, "I feel ashamed." This was the beginning of humanity having their clothes say something about them.

The process of imputing meaning into something is more a matter of *perception* than it is of *calculation*. There isn't a set universal formula that can be used to assess the meaning of something. Everyone projects or interprets meaning based on the perception of what either they themselves or what others have said the meaning of something is. From that perception we associate a value to many of the things we find to be meaningful.

For instance, I can look at a painting that an art critic has determined not to be valuable because it doesn't meet some standard of what the critic says is essential for a painting to be considered beautiful. However, if I look deeply at that painting and it captures *my* attention, and I feel the painting is actually looking into *my* eyes and dialoguing with *my* memories, emotions, and feelings to find harmony with me and establishing meaning, then the painting becomes beautiful to me. When the criticized painting does this to me, I assign a value to the painting based on the meaning of what makes it beautiful to me, regardless of what the critic says about it. The same can be said of a score of music, an exquisitely crafted sculpture, nature itself, and even clothing. All these things can speak a language to us of its meaning that words may be able to neither express nor interpret.

Whenever there is communication between people—either verbally or non-verbally, an interpretation of the message being communicated is always involved. This is referred to as *hermeneutics*, which is the theory and methodology of interpretation. In Greek mythology, Hermes was known as the messenger of the gods. His job was to communicate messages that the gods sent to each other and to humans. He was attributed as being the inventor of language and speech, and he served as an interpreter of communication. He was also known to be a liar, a thief, and a trickster. This is why the interpretation of communication is called "hermeneutics" because the way a message being sent and/or the interpretation of that message can be deceiving.

Socrates indicated that words had the power to both reveal meaning and conceal it. The same is true for non-verbal communication such as the messages clothes can send to both the wearer and the onlooker when they are worn. You can either intentionally or unintentionally send a message through the clothing you wear. Others interpret that message by assigning their own meaning to the message being received based on what they think the message is that you are trying to send through your clothing.

From the first time Adam and Eve draped fig leaves over their bodies to express their feeling of shame, clothing has come to represent and express a variety of meanings. Clothing can communicate the social class you belong to (or that you want people to think you belong to), the status you hold (or the status you want people to think that you hold), or your specific role or duty you play or perform (or the one you want people to think you have). The first item to have a message attributed to it, to symbolize that message, and then communicate the message to another person without having to communicate it actively, consciously, or verbally is clothing.

CLOTHING LAYER #2:
MID-LAYER

THE POWER OF CLOTHES

In August of 1897, Mark Twain wrote in one of his personal notebooks: "Strip the human race, absolutely naked, and it would be a real democracy. But the introduction of even a rag of a tiger skin, or a cow tail, could make a badge of distinction and be the beginning of a monarchy." Reduce humanity to a state where we're all in our natural uniform and we embody no added visible distinctions and express none of our individuality, personal uniqueness, positions of power, or personality traits through bodily decoration, and we are all equal.

Soliloquy № 7

Twain later included the above quote from his notebook in an article he published entitled "The Czar's Soliloquy" in an edition of the journal *The North American Review*. He expounded on this thought in the form of a story. It began with an epigram that framed the narrative: "After the Czar's morning bath it is his habit to meditate an hour before dressing himself—*London Times Correspondence*." Through the voice of the Czar of Russia, Twain wrote the following narrative:

> [Viewing himself in the pier-glass.] Naked, what am I? A lank, skinny, spider-legged libel on the image of God! Look at the waxwork head—the face, with the expression of a melon—the projecting ears—the knotted elbows—the dished breast—the knife-edged shins—and then the feet, all beads and joints and bone-sprays, an imitation X-ray photograph! There is nothing imperial about this, nothing imposing, nothing impressive, nothing to invoke awe and reverence. Is it this that a hundred and forty million Russians kiss the dust before and worship? Manifestly not! No one could worship this spectacle which is Me. Then who is it, what is it that they worship? Privately, none knows better than I: it is my clothes. Without my clothes I should be as destitute of authority as any other naked person. Nobody could tell me from a parson, a barber, a dude. Then who is the real Emperor of Russia? My clothes. There is no other.
>
> As Teufelsdröckh suggested, what would man be—what would *any* man be—without his clothes? As soon as one stops and thinks over that proposition, one realizes that without his clothes a man would be nothing at all; that the clothes do not merely make the man, the clothes

Clothing Layer #2: MID-LAYER

are the man; that without him he is a cipher, a vacancy, a nobody, a nothing.

Titles—another artificiality—are a part of his clothing. They and the dry good conceal the wearer's inferiority and make him seem great and a wonder, when at bottom there is nothing remarkable about him. They can move a nation to fall on its knees and sincerely worship an Emperor, who without the clothes and the title, would drop to the rank of the cobbler and be swallowed up and lost sight of in the massed multitude of the inconsequentials; an Emperor who, naked in the naked world, would get no notice, excite no remark, and be heedlessly shouldered and jostled like any other certified stranger, and perhaps offered a kopek to carry somebody's gripsack; yet an Emperor who, by the sheer might of those artificialities—clothes and a title—can get himself worshipped as a deity by his people, and at his pleasure and unrebuked can exile them, hunt them, harry them, destroy them, just as he would with so many rats if the accident of birth had furnished him a calling better suited to his capacities than empering. It is a stupendous force—that which resides in the all-concealing cloak of clothes and title; they fill the onlooker with awe; they make him tremble; yet he knows that every hereditary regal dignity commemorates a usurpation, a power illegitimately acquired, an authority conveyed and conferred by persons who did not own it. For monarchs have been chosen and elected by aristocracies only: a Nation has never elected one.

Soliloquy № 7

There is no power without clothes. It is the power that governs the human race. Strip its chiefs to the skin, and no State could be governed; naked officials could exercise no authority; they would look (and be) like everybody else—commonplace, inconsequential. A policeman in plain clothes is one man; in his uniform he is ten. Clothes and title are the most potent thing, the most formidable influence, in the earth. They move the human race to willing and spontaneous respect for the judge, the general, the admiral, the bishop, the ambassador, the frivolous earl, the idiot duke, the sultan, the king, the emperor. No great title is efficient without clothes to support it. In naked tribes of savages, the kings wear some kind of rag or decoration which they make sacred to themselves and allow no one else to wear. The king of the great Fan tribe wears a bit of leopard-skin on his shoulder—it is sacred to royalty; the rest of him is perfectly naked. Without his bit of leopard-skin to awe and impress the people, he would not be able to keep his job...To think this thing in the mirror—this vegetable—is an accepted deity to a mighty nation, an innumerable host, and nobody laughs; and at the same time is a diligent and practical professional devil, and nobody marvels, nobody murmurs about incongruities and inconsistencies! Is the human race a joke? Was it devised and patched together in a dull time when there was nothing important to do? Has it no respect for itself? ...I think my respect for it is drooping, sinking—and my respect for myself along with it...There is but one restorative—*Clothes*! respect-reviving, spirit-uplifting clothes! heaven's kindest gift to man, his only protection against finding himself out: they deceive him, they confer dignity upon him; without them he has none. How charitable are clothes, how beneficent, how puissant, how inestimably precious! Mine are able to expand a human cipher into a globe-shadowing portent; they can command the respect of the whole world—including my own, which is fading. I will put them on.

Twain's story illustrates the power clothes have on the way others view and treat us. He also points out some of the effects that enclothed cognition has on us. At the end of the story, he says that clothes are "heaven's kindest gift to man, his only protection against finding himself out: they deceive him, they confer dignity upon him; without them he has none." Twain was talking about clothes that have significant meaning associated with them. I don't believe the Czar could have put on a long T-shirt and some ripped skinny jeans and still felt the same way that his emperor clothes made him feel.

RETRO CLOTHING

Throughout history, many observations have been made about the effects that clothes have had on the viewer as well as on the wearer. In the year AD 1500—four hundred years before Twain's story had been published, a Dutch Catholic priest named Erasmus scoured vast amounts of ancient literature to compile a collection of Greek and Latin proverbs. He published them in his work *Adagia Chiliades*.

One of the Latin proverbs he found was, "Vestis virum facit," which means, "Clothes make the man." This statement has since become a maxim for modern purveyors of gentleman's attire, but it accurately portrays the effect that enclothed cognition has on the wearer of clothing.

The Roman speaker Marcus Fabius Quintilianus (better known as "Quintilian") penned a twelve-volume textbook on rhetoric in the year AD 95 entitled *Institutio Oratoria*, or "Institutes of Oratory." In it, he wrote, "To dress within the formal limits and with an air gives men, as the Greek line testifies, authority."

Homer, the Greek writer who authored the epic story *Odyssey* sometime between 8-7 BC said, "From these things [appearance], you may be sure, men get a good report." Homer also wrote, "At first, I thought his [Ulysses] appearance was unseemly, but now he has the air of the gods who dwell in the wide heaven."

The Devil Wears Prada

Between 593-571 BC, the prophet Ezekiel—under the inspiration of the Holy Spirit—wrote down what God had spoken to an angel named Lucifer. Lucifer appeared to have had the "air of the gods who dwell in the wide heaven" because of the clothes he was wearing. In the book of Ezekiel, God was indirectly talking to the fallen angel (as he was known to do throughout Scripture) by addressing him through the King of Tyre. Everything Ezekiel wrote could have easily been spoken to an earthly ruler, but it's clear that what was written down was addressed to one who was above the realm of humanity:

> Son of man, sing this funeral song for the king of Tyre. Give him this message from the Sovereign LORD: "You were the model of perfection, full of wisdom and exquisite in beauty. You were in Eden, the garden of God. Your clothing was adorned with every precious stone—red

carnelian, pale-green peridot, white moonstone, blue-green beryl, onyx, green jasper, blue lapis lazuli, turquoise, and emerald—all beautifully crafted for you and set in the finest gold. They were given to you on the day you were created. I ordained and anointed you as the mighty angelic guardian. You had access to the holy mountain of God and walked among the stones of fire. You were blameless in all you did from the day you were created until the day evil was found in you. Your rich commerce led you to violence, and you sinned. So I banished you in disgrace from the mountain of God. I expelled you, O mighty guardian, from your place among the stones of fire. Your heart was filled with pride because of all your beauty. Your wisdom was corrupted by your love of splendor. So, I threw you to the ground and exposed you to the curious gaze of kings."[1]

Lucifer may very well have been the first created being to have been affected by the powerful influence that clothing can have on its wearer through enclothed cognition. From the time of his creation, Lucifer was clothed like no other angel; pride entered his heart because of his beauty. His clothing, which was a major contributor to his beauty, was intended to communicate to all who gazed upon him that God is creation's perfecter. The effect that enclothed cognition had on Lucifer was that his clothes made him *feel* as if he was a perfect creation. Lucifer's beauty was the result of God's creation, but it became the cause of Lucifer's pride.

Twain was on to something when he wrote that we're nothing without the meaning clothes give to us. The "curious

---

1. Ezekiel 28:12-17

gaze of kings" upon Lucifer might have been the result of the removal of his clothes of splendor. He was exposed by God, and the kings saw Lucifer for who he really was without God.

Choosing What to Wear

From the most powerful angelic being to the most helpless human infant, clothing involves choice. For both, clothing was chosen by someone else for them to wear. There are still facets of almost every culture where clothing choice is made by someone other than the wearer. There are private and public schools that require students to wear school uniforms. Inmates in the prison system are issued jumpsuits or scrubs to wear, much like soldiers who serve in the military are issued their branch's version of the Battle Dress Uniform (BDU). Many blue-collar jobs have uniform apparel chosen by their company's corporate executives. Sports teams parade around in identical jerseys that identify them as a member of their team's franchise. And (to a degree) many corporate positions require that men wear a suit and tie while women wear a dress or skirt. Clothing choices are sometimes made by someone other than the wearer.

This brings us to the question, "What influences us as church leaders—many having the freedom to wear whatever we want to wear—to choose the clothes we will cover our bodies with while we lead our church or ministry?" The expectations of church congregations as well as historical traditions previously established what church leaders wear. With traditional ecclesial vestments (such as robes, collars, chimeres, surplices, cinctures, tippets, and even suits), significant meaning has been associated with the clothing being worn by the minister—much like a doctor's white lab coat.

Times have changed, and time has also eroded many church traditions, including ministerial vestments. So, what now influences the minister or ministry leader in their choice of clothing as many (if not most) can make clothing choices for themselves?

Clothing with Character

Professor David Riesman wrote what was considered by many to be the most influential book of the twentieth century for understanding society in America. In his influential book *The Lonely Crowd* he identified Americans as belonging to three different social character types. The book was instrumental in causing readers to begin characterizing others into one of these three types. At the same time, readers also began to discover themselves as fitting into one of these three types.

There are those whom Riesman characterized as *tradition-directed*. These tend to adhere to the rules "dictated to a very large degree by power relations among the various age and sex groups, the clans, castes, professions—relations which have endured for centuries and are modified but slightly, if at all, by successive generations." This means that their tendency to follow tradition is what insured their conformity to the expectations set forth by tradition. This type of person would hardly think of themselves as an individual.

Inner-directed types developed the capacity to go at it alone, apart from tradition and conformed to an internalized set of their own expectations. This type would initially go against the grain, not having much regard for tradition as they based their values on a separate set of goals. These goals included the creation of beauty from their own perceptions. They had gained a feeling of control over their own lives and would hardly think about themselves in light of tradition.

Less dynamic than the inner-directed character type was the *other-directed* individual. They were sensitized to the expectations and preferences of others and conformed to those expectations to be accepted into the mainstream. Riesman writes,

> What is common to all the other-directed people is that their contemporaries are the source of direction for the individual—either those known to him or those with whom he is indirectly acquainted, through friends and through the mass media...While all people want and need to be liked by some of the people some of the time, it is only the modern other-directed types who make this their chief source of direction and chief area of sensitivity.

Ministry leaders can still use these three social characterizations to better understand how our clothes end up acquiring significant meaning. We can also begin to observe how our clothing influences our actions and behaviors. These character types are beneficial as they supply another lens to examine how we express our own imagination to others through our clothing choices.

Tradition-Directed Clothing

For centuries, leaders in the church have adhered to a tradition-directed approach regarding the clothing to be worn while ministering. Personal choice had never been an option. From the priestly vestments that began to be worn during the time of the Old Testament tabernacle to the late twentieth century when suits and ties were commonly being worn by mainline ministers, church leaders have worn clothing that has traditionally had significant meaning.

The significance of priestly clothing was first given by God as he instructed Moses to institute the priesthood to serve the people of Israel at the tabernacle. God told Moses to make different clothing for the priests than the clothes worn by the common Israelite. Thus, the adoption of a tradition-directed approach to what church leaders wore had begun by God himself.

God took great care in ordering every detail in the establishment of his tabernacle. He even had the clothing that the priests would wear created for a specific purpose. It would appear the purpose was two-fold: (1) so the priests would personally possess dignity and honor for the priestly role while wearing the clothes, and (2) that the people would give honor both to God and to the role and office of the priesthood as ministers in God's tabernacle. Both the priests and the people were to be conscious of the sacred role God's Church and his ministers played in the community.

God told Moses to gather Aaron and his sons to serve him as priests in the tabernacle. Moses was twice given specific instructions as to the garments that he must make for the priests to wear as they served in their priestly roles.[1] In both verses where this command was recorded it states that the reason God gave the priests clothing that was different from those who were not in leadership in the tabernacle was "to give them dignity and honor."

The common Israelite was forbidden from wearing the same fabric mixture of linen and wool in their clothes. Only the priestly garments and the tabernacle weavings themselves were to be made of that mixture.[2] There was to be a visible distinction between the priesthood and the neighborhood. This was a continued practice until a new covenant would be made in the death, burial, and resurrection of Jesus Christ. God told

---

1. Exodus 28:2, Exodus 28:40 (NIV)
2. Deuteronomy 22:11

Moses, "This shall be a lasting ordinance for Aaron and his descendants."[1]

Enclothed cognition would influence the priests as they performed their functions. They would be more mindful of their duties and act with dignity and reverence while wearing the special clothing. The people who saw the priests wearing these sacred clothes would be mindful to give honor and respect to God. They would also give honor and respect to those who ministered before God as his priests. This became a tradition-directed means of ascribing significant meaning to clothing.

Let me pause here with a few questions: How many modern church leaders would be willing to submit to a tradition-directed approach to our ministry apparel as some faith traditions continue to do? Do the apparel choices of church leaders in the twenty-first century still confer dignity and honor upon the ministers who serve as "modernized" leaders in the church as they once did? Did the priestly garments help those ministering in the tabernacle to have more reverence for God and for their role? Does the clothing of modern culture worn by today's ministers help promote dignity and honor as we minister for God and to his people? Does the clothing of modern culture worn by today's ministers help to promote dignity and honor given by the people for God and his ministers?

Tzitziyot

In the book of Numbers, God instructed Moses to tell the people of Israel to "Make tassels on the corners of their garments throughout their generations, and to put a cord of blue on the tassel of each corner."[2] These tassels (called *tzitziyot*) would be a visible reminder for Israel to both remember and keep

---

1. Deuteronomy 22:43
2. Numbers 15:38-40

Clothing Layer #2: MID-LAYER

God's commandments and not to follow their own hearts and eyes. These tassels had significant meaning attributed to them and were a type of ideogram that communicated this meaning to the people of Israel through enclothed cognition.

During this time, non-Jews of noble rank wore tassels to signify their nobility. For the Jews to wear tassels, it would be a reminder to them that they belonged to the House of God and were his noble children. They were set apart from the neighborhood of other people. The blue dye used for the cord in the tassels was the same blue dye used in the making of both the high priest's robe and the tabernacle covering. They were even made from a wool-linen mix—the same combination as the fabric of the priests' clothing and the tabernacle.[1] The tassels were to symbolize to the common Israelite that they themselves were like their tassels—a combination of nobility and priesthood.

These tassels communicated to all of Israel that they had the same status as a priest—they ministered to the world on behalf of God and did so with dignity and honor. When an Israelite wore the tassels, the effect of enclothed cognition caused them to view themselves as being of nobility and not as merely a slave set free. Additionally, their behavior was to be in a manner that functioned in accordance with the priesthood. The tassels embodied the same meaning for the rest of the Israelites as the ceremonial clothing did for the priests.

From Holy Clothing to "Holey" Clothing

After the Day of Pentecost and during the first century up until the fourth century, the Church was being established under the New Covenant in both Jewish and Gentile communities.

---

1. The tassels were not clothing, but accessories attached to their clothing so they would not be violating the command given by God in Deuteronomy 22:11.

Soliloquy № 7

The Jewish leaders of the newly-established Christian Church appear to have been wearing ordinary clothes that were no different from what everyone else was wearing. The indication that an individual served as a minister in the church when the congregation was assembled was not signified by the clothing they wore.

Perhaps Jewish Christians began dressing like everyone else by not wearing tassels on the corners of their clothing because Christians were being persecuted at that time. It wouldn't have been wise for any Christian who also observed Jewish traditions to distinguish themselves from those who were non-religious—and especially as a church leader. In fact, all Jewish Christians might have begun to dress without wearing tassels and in an ordinary manner to keep from drawing attention to themselves and being persecuted. It could also be that they stopped wearing tassels on the corners of their clothing because of the teaching that the law had been fulfilled in the New Covenant with Christ.

A Jew wearing the tasseled *haluk* which went underneath the clothing with the tassels hanging down might have caused Roman persecutors to question them as to whether they were a Christian. To avoid persecution, the tassels were sewn to a rectangular mantle or prayer shawl called a *tallit* that could be worn over the clothes and be easily removed. For someone who was non-Jewish and had become a Christian, their clothing had never been a factor that identified them as being religious.

The Church continued to expand into the fourth century when Christianity was legalized under Constantine. Distinguished articles of clothing would again come to signify an individual as a church leader. Ministers began to dress in either one of two ways: (1) a bright scarf, a long tunic, or a handkerchief was conferred upon a church leader by the state, symbolizing their clerical status, or (2) church leaders preserved the ancient Roman way of dressing by wearing the more traditional "ordinary" clothes. These would eventually become stylized as the distinctive clothing worn by church leadership.

Clothing Layer #2: MID-LAYER

Clergy vestments would continue to evolve until the Reformation. Traditional, clerical clothing began to be rejected by ministers of the Reformed and Presbyterian churches. Huldrych Zwingli, a leader of the Reformation in Switzerland, abolished the wearing of all clothing that distinguished members of the clergy. John Calvin, a French pastor/reformer ministering in Geneva during the Protestant Reformation, began to wear what would have been considered during that time to be outdoor clothing as he performed his ministerial duties in the church.

Time passed into the twentieth century, and large numbers of ministers literally "followed suit" by conducting their services and duties wearing dark business suits. Riesman would have identified this as a shift away from a tradition-directed towards an inner-directed approach to choosing clothing. Interestingly, as these church leaders were breaking away from the old traditional vestments associated with church leadership, the clothing style they adopted merely became the contemporary traditional vestments worn by church leaders. The suit came to be what church leaders would wear to minister in their churches rather than scarves, tunics, or robes. Whereas clerical clothing used to be prescribed to church leaders (tradition-directed), the suit now became the clerical clothing preferred by church leaders (inner-directed).

As we moved closer to the twenty-first century, church leaders progressively began to break away from wearing a suit and tie (or from wearing a dress as more women began to be accepted as church leaders). Professional business clothing had been the contemporary traditional vestments that church leaders wore. It has now become increasingly impossible to distinguish the leaders of the church from the members of the church. Likewise, church members are indistinguishable from those in society who don't belong to the church. Church leaders used to dress differently to identify themselves as church leaders, and church members used to put on their best for church to distinguish the Sabbath day from the work week.

It used to be that on a Sunday you could tell who had gone to church (and speculate that they were Christians) because Christians were the only ones wearing nice clothes on a Sunday. In today's culture, however, it now appears that many church members dress more casually for church than they are required to dress for work. People now appear to "remember the work week and keep it holy, and remember the sabbath and keep it *holey*."

As a result, church and ministry leaders seem to have followed the lead of culture and done the same. The clothing church attendees now wear has ceased to serve as an indicator of their respect for the Lord's Day and the House of God. Likewise, clothing has also ceased to serve as a symbol of the minister's respect for their position of leadership. Of course, this isn't the case for every faith tradition. Many church members still consciously wear their best when they go to church as do some church leaders when they minister. Dr. Tony Evans, Bishop T.D. Jakes, Ravi Zacharias, and Joel Osteen come to mind.

Those who are Jewish—God's chosen people—are dedicated to their faith and they still honor the commands of their tradition. Many still wear the tzitzit to identify themselves as (and perhaps remind them that they are) God's "chosen ones." The rest of us who are Christians—God's adopted people—don't wear any such visible identifiers or reminders that we belong to God (except for well-meaning Christian T-shirts sold by companies that have Christian spins on modern slogans or brands).

COMMON THREADS

So, if enclothed cognition were to have the effect of causing a church leader to think, act, and behave differently when traditional, more professional clothes are worn, our culture seems to have stripped a growing number of ministers of those clothes. When it comes to how ministry leaders choose their clothes and what they want their clothing to say both *to* them and *about* them, some ministers have undoubtedly become what Riesman would characterize as "outer-directed." If you recall, this is the character type that would make clothing choices based on the preferences and expectations of those whom they wish to be accepted by.

Has the desire by ministers to bridge the priesthood with the neighborhood contributed to the diminished view of the role and function of church leadership in the eyes of the people in the church and in our society? Has it also diminished the role and function of church leadership in our *own* eyes? Some leaders within the modern church may try to justify dressing in the same fashion trends of popular culture rather than in clothes that have traditionally been associated with leadership. Allow me to explore this idea a bit.

Professional Ministers

Throughout medieval and early modern history, there were only three fields of work that were acknowledged as being a profession: the theological profession, the medical profession, and the legal profession—the three "learned professions." There was no such thing as a professional athlete, a professional singer, or a professional gamer as we have come to call anything that someone does to make a living today. In fact, up through the eleventh century, theology was considered to be the *only* recognized profession. It was not until the twelfth and thirteenth centuries that medicine and law joined the ranks of the professions as a course of study within the university curriculum.

These three professions each exhibit the five core characteristics of a profession. These characteristics have served as a measure of what constituted any field of work to be considered a profession: (1) prolonged, specialized intellectual training (2) institutional or scientific technique (3) remuneration for professional service (4) a sense of responsibility to the client, and (5) a professional culture sustained by the formation of associations.

According to Ernest Greenwood and his book *The Elements of Professionalization*, a professional culture has social values and norms specific to its profession. These include the way one dresses. Doctors continue to wear their white lab coats to differentiate themselves from nurses and visitors; Judges, their black judicial robes. The reason that these two original learned professions continue to do so is partly because of tradition. They have kept the professional culture of their formed associations by preserving the tradition of their dress since the twelfth and thirteenth century (respectively).

Ashamedly, when it comes to the original profession of theology, it appears it's the only one of the three professions that has broken from tradition regarding the expectations of dress and of keeping a professional culture. While some faith traditions keep their traditional dress codes of the past, many others have abandoned them. When ministers choose to wear the trending clothing styles of the day, they cease to be seen as a professional when compared to doctors and lawyers. This has the long-term effect of our society ceasing to view ministry as a respectable profession, and ministers as professionals.

When people are serious about making an impression on people they hope will take them seriously, they dress according to the level of respect they have for those individuals, and/or to gain their respect. At one time, young men and women would wear the best clothes they had to go on a date. This was an outward display of the inner respect they had for themselves, for the other person, and for the honor of being asked to (or having the young lady agree to) spend time with each another exclusively. It was also a surface-level way for the

Clothing Layer #2: MID-LAYER

guy to communicate to the girl's parents that he respected their daughter and considered it an honor for them to allow him to take her out. To use an iron and get dressed up was the least a guy could do to show he respected the young lady and was himself, respectable.

When a wedding couple wears a wedding gown and a tuxedo (respectively) on their wedding day, they do so to show the mutual respect they have for one another. Each wants to be considered by the other's family and friends as either being a beautiful bride or a respectable gentleman as well. By dressing their absolute best, the couple shows that the exchanging of vows (vows which are supposed to come with a lifetime warranty) isn't an ordinary event but an extraordinary one.

When making an appearance in court, plaintiffs and defendants dress up to present themselves as respectable, responsible citizens—even if they actually aren't. Not only does dressing up show respect for the judge, but it's intended to serve as an indicator that the individual takes their court appearance seriously. Dressing up is often highly suggested by lawyers for the reasons said above, but they know it can also have a psychological impact on the jury. Lawyers will coach their clients to present themselves in the best way possible—verbally, non-verbally, and visibly—to positively influence the jury to decide in their favor (the jury's judgement would have begun to be influenced when they first looked at them).

The overwhelming majority of leaders who work in the legal and medical professions continue to dress professionally as they traditionally have out of respect for their profession, their clientele, and perhaps, themselves. Why is it then that the trend for a growing number of church and ministry leaders in the theological profession—namely among emerging Evangelical Protestants—seems to be wearing whatever clothing is currently being worn in mainstream culture?

Soliloquy № 7

CLOTHING LAYER #3:
OUTER LAYER

In this last layer, I will present three arguments I've encountered which could be made in favor of updating the church or ministry leader's professional wardrobe to the latest fashion trends.

Argument #1: *"I want to create a RELAXED atmosphere in our church/ministry where no one will feel judged for what they are wearing."*

My wife and I once attended a large church that had a coat room. Upon entering the church, you could check your coat the same way you would as if you went to the opera or an upscale restaurant. While looking at all the outerwear that had been checked, I saw more wool and fur than Noah had on board the Ark. If someone were to have gone to this church and didn't have on a suit or a dress they would have felt out of place. While none of the church's members intentionally came for a fashion show, or to be noticed by others for what they were wearing, those who didn't regularly attend that church could easily have felt as if they were in an environment where they would be judged by members for what they were or were not wearing.

When people began keeping their suits and dresses on the hanger in their own closets and "relaxed" the style of clothing they wore to church, many ministers began dressing the way the people who came to their church were dressing. Some ministers might have even led their congregations in this practice rather than following the lead of their members and relaxed the style of clothing they wore while ministering.

First, some (male) ministers began to preach in a suit but without a tie, or wore a tie but without the suit coat. In place of a dress or skirt, some (female) ministers began to wear

Clothing Layer #3: OUTER LAYER

dress slacks (I remember when my sister who is a worship pastor began to lead worship wearing dress slacks underneath a skirt as Darlene Zschech, the worship leader at the time at Hillsong Church in Australia, had been doing). The progressive "relaxing" of what is worn to minister has continued, and the degree of relaxed clothing varies by context—it ranges from Hawaiian shirts and sandals or ripped jeans and hoodies to skin-tight leggings and oversized T-shirts.

So, let me see if I understand this rationale correctly: If *everyone* in the church is wearing the "uniform of the culture" rather than the "uniform of the church," we can *all* relax, knowing that no one within the walls of the church will be judging one another, right?

Perhaps at one point some church leaders had been listening to those who didn't feel comfortable going to church (like the one I mentioned above) and discovered why they didn't. One of the excuses "outsiders" might have given was that they didn't want to get all dressed up to go to church, or that they didn't have any "church clothes." This would cause the non-attender to feel as though they were being judged, which would naturally make anyone feel uncomfortable.

I get it.

For the most part, our American culture doesn't provide many opportunities for us to get dressed up anymore. The suit or dress hanging in the closet may get worn to a wedding, funeral, or graduation ceremony—rare occasions. As a result, church leaders might have responded to this cultural reality by "relaxing the dress code" for these people so they would no longer have a valid excuse for not going to church.

Point taken.

All church leaders want people to come as they are and not feel as though they are being judged. But regardless of what church-goers wear, there still seems to be this persistent idea that Christians are judgmental. The fact of the matter is: *all* humans are judgmental—not just Christians.

Soliloquy № 7

When unbelievers state that the reason they don't go to church is because Christians are judgmental, they are being just as judgmental as the Christians they are condemning for being judgmental! When someone who doesn't go to church comes through the doors of our ministry with the preconceived belief that they'll be judged by those in the church for what they are wearing, they themselves have already passed judgment on the people in the church. Oftentimes, it's the unbeliever who is more judgmental than the believer, but they wouldn't want to admit it.

This doesn't excuse a Christian's behavior. The way many Christians act inside of the church isn't any different from the way they act outside of it. The Church can do all it wants inside of the church building to try to reduce the stigma of Christians being judgmental. But unless the Church behaves in a non-judgmental way *outside* of the church building, the perception that people have of the Church isn't going to be changed by the way church leaders or their congregations dress. We're just "wolves in sheep's clothing"[1] if we are going to dress like the culture but not act differently from it. What good is it to be absolved of being judgmental only to be condemned of hypocrisy?

Judgements are made based on outward appearances as we have previously discussed. Sometimes we overestimate the importance of our appearance, both when we underdress and when we overdress. Australian newscaster Karl Stefanovic once drew attention to this. He wanted to point out how people are often more critical of the way females dress than the way males dress. His female co-host was constantly being bombarded with criticisms and suggestions about her outward appearance and wardrobe, so he conducted his own personal experiment by wearing the exact same suit for their television broadcast for an entire year. At the end of the year, when he had been asked about the results of his experiment, he said,

---

1. Matthew 7:15

> No one has noticed; no one gives a s**t. But when women wear the wrong colour and they get pulled up. They say the wrong thing and there's thousands of tweets written about them. Women are judged much more harshly and keenly for what they do, what they say and what they wear.
>
> I've worn the same suit on air for a year—except for a couple of times because of circumstances—to make a point. I'm judged on my interviews, my appalling sense of humour—on how I do my job, basically. Whereas women are quite often judged on what they're wearing or how their hair is...that's [what I wanted to test].

The point of this newscaster's experiment was to illuminate the fact that people made judgments against the female newscaster based on her appearance while never once making a comment on his appearance. Conversely, people judged his work performance while the female never once received comments on her job performance. Even in terms of a man searching for a potential partner in a romantic relationship, research shows that men immediately judge women based on their appearance while women take longer to decide because their decisions are largely based on a man's character.[1] Give these thoughts some consideration:

> (1) It appears that the reason being given for ministers dressing in a way that's relaxed, in vogue, and gives the

---

1. Johanna C. Van Hooff, Helen Crawford, and Mark Van Vugt, "The Wandering Mind of Men: ERP Evidence for Gender Differences in Attention Bias towards Attractive opposite Sex Faces," *Social Cognitive and Affective Neuroscience* 6.4 (2010): 477-85.

appearance of being non-judgmental to an unbelieving audience, is being postulated by male church leaders.
(2) The vast majority of church and ministry leaders are male.
(3) Males are genetically programmed to make judgements about people based on their appearance which may explain why the trend of ministers dressing to fit in with the clothing styles of culture is so heavily promoted.
(4) Male ministry leaders are giving more attention than female ministry leaders are to the idea that unbelievers might perceive ministers and the ministries they lead as being judgmental based on appearance.

These insights may reveal why modern church leaders are giving more attention to how we look to an outside audience rather than creating and seeking out opportunities to personally interact with unbelievers so our Christ-like character and qualities can be revealed. It may be that male church leaders are projecting their gender-associated judgment bias onto others, assuming everyone judges the Church and its leaders based on appearance.

If we want to curb our culture away from labelling the Church as being judgmental and communicate that we accept people just as they are, we need to spend more time building relationships with people outside of the church and less time building our modern wardrobe in hopes that what we wear inside the church will do the job.

Since it takes less effort to look at what culture is wearing outwardly and emulate it than it does to get outside of the church and build relationships with those within our culture, human nature will have us travel the easier path. What the world needs is for church leaders to spend less time in our clothes closet and trying to visually influence people, and to spend more time in our prayer closet along with personally influencing people through forged relationships.

Clothing Layer #3: OUTER LAYER

Slip into Something More Comfortable

An attempt by leaders to disarm the perception the world has of Christians being judgmental was made when both the minister and church members began wearing more relaxed "Saturday" clothes to church. But what else might church leaders end up relaxing for people to feel comfortable once they come to our churches?

An article in the newspaper *USA Today* entitled "Most Religious Groups in USA Have Lost Ground, Survey Finds" cites a quote from Mark Silk, director of the Greenberg Center for the Study of Religion in Public Life at Trinity College that offers some insight. In the article, Silk suggested that he saw "an emergence of a soft evangelicalism—E-lite—that owes a lot to evangelical styles of worship and basic approach to church. But E-lite is more a matter of aesthetic and style and a considerable softening of the edges in doctrine, politics, and social values."

First, we relax our clothes to make people feel comfortable. Then, we must relax our convictions to *keep* them comfortable. If we make it past the hurdle of not making people feel judged based on appearances, won't they find that the gospel we believe "cuts all the way into us, where the soul and spirit are joined…and it judges the thoughts and feelings in our hearts"?[1] Might they continue labelling us as judgmental once they discover that our beliefs and worldviews don't coincide with theirs? If we've relaxed our style of dress to accommodate an unbelieving world, it's also possible that we'll end up relaxing our doctrine to continue accommodating them so

---

1. Hebrews 4:12-13 (NCV)

Soliloquy № 7

they'll like us and not view us as being judgmental. This is a clear case of the "tail wagging the dog."[1]

The enemy has tactics that work to keep people from having an encounter with God. Satan would love nothing more than to use the Church itself to keep people from encountering God. Our good intentions can backfire and leave the Church needing its fire back unless we remain vigilant. If church leaders aren't careful, we won't know where to draw the line between relaxing what we wear and what we believe.

Are we ministry leaders still serious about the mission we've been given by God, or are we finished attempting to fulfill it under the power and influence of the Holy Spirit? Is it time for us to take off our work clothes and relax? In the folly of our human thinking, we might have adopted "relaxation" as a strategy to fulfill God's mission for the church. But the long game seems to have more Christians in the church remaining in a relaxed state rather than engaging in a relentless pursuit of the mission of God.

Oh sure, there are lots of people volunteering when there's an organized ministry opportunity prepared for them to participate in. The church supplies a cause or need and a matching T-shirt for them to wear while serving. There's a start and end time, and participants get to keep the T-shirt that advertises to others they did something to impact the world for the Kingdom of God. But the church shouldn't have to provide its members with a cause and a T-shirt before people are called to action. God has already given us a "be-*cause*." We're supposed to *be* living in the *cause*!

All around believers are causes and needs that—if they're looking—present themselves *outside* of the church every day. "Be-cause" God loved the world in its sinful condition, he gave

---

1. People talk about **the tail wagging the dog** to describe a situation where an unimportant part of something or an unimportant person or group involved in something has too much influence over it.

his only Son to leave the comforts of Heaven and go to the world to *be*-in-the-*cause* and save it.

Those we lead must be in the cause every moment of their lives. God's *'cause* is for them to be salt and light in the world. Ministry must be more than having people wait for organized opportunities that the church provides for them to participate in so they can help us accomplish our plans. There's a tremendous need for believers to be *in* the cause and not just be there *for* the cause. Cause is everywhere! The cause for church leaders is to equip and resource those whom we lead so they can accomplish God's purpose for their lives.[1]

The Church can't be in a relaxed state until there is a scheduled opportunity to *put on* a T-shirt and serve. Believers must always be in a relentless state of mind and ready —eyes wide open to the needs around them—looking for an opportunity to *give* the T-shirt off their back, not waiting for an opportunity to put one on. While it's great to be "shirt-wearers" together when serving the needs of others in scheduled times of organized ministry, believers must also be "shirt-sharers" when needs spontaneously present themselves in the unscheduled times of our daily lives.

Rather than make our churches and ministries more sensitive to seekers who *enter* the doors of the church, we must encourage those whom we lead to become more sensitive to people who are seeking when they *exit* the doors of the church. *Seeking is the job of the Church, not the job of the disinterested.* If the Church wants to project the image that we're not judgmental, then we should actually *be* non-judgmental when we interact with the world outside of the church. "Be wise in the way you act towards outsiders. Make the most of every opportunity."[2]

---

1. Ephesians 4:11-12

2. Colossians 4:5 (NIV)

Soliloquy № 7

Remember Who You Are Working For

Shouldn't we, as servants of God, be more concerned about honoring the Master of the House than we are about catering to the whims of those on the guest list whom he's invited to come to his House? Church leaders serve God first and *then* we lead his people. If we serve people first, we end up leading God to where we feel he's needed most. Ministers should be the runway models that create a culture of reverence for God and his House. Charles Spurgeon wrote in his devotional book *Morning and Evening*:

> Before my conversion, I could...go to God's house and pretend to pray to him and praise him [which] argues a brazen-facedness of the worst kind! Alas! Since the day of my new birth I have...worshipped before him in a slovenly[1] manner...I should have far more holy fear, and a far deeper contrition of spirit.

My pastor often says that the spiritual mirrors the physical, and the physical mirrors the spiritual. This means the condition of our inward spiritual life often manifests itself outwardly in our physical life. This goes both ways. The condition of our physical life is often manifested inwardly through our spiritual life. If this saying has any truth to it (which I strongly feel it does), what does our outward appearance reveal about our inward spiritual life? And how is our inward spiritual life *affected* by our outward appearance? I know that man looks on the outward appearance and God looks at the heart,[2] but as

---

1. Slovenly is defined as being untidy or unclean especially in personal appearance or habits.

2. 1 Samuel 16:7

God changes the heart, the outward life should begin to reflect those inward changes.

Paul illustrates this concept by using the analogy of a bride wearing the most dazzling outfit as she stands before her husband-to-be. He writes that Christ cleansed the Church so he could present her to himself in *splendor* without spot or wrinkle.[1] Herein lies the point being made regarding enclothed cognition: when I wear my best as a leader in the service of God, I am conscious of the fact that *I am the bride of Christ*, preparing both myself and those I minister to here on earth to be presented to Christ in heaven. Regardless of how others may choose to dress, as a leader in God's Kingdom we should represent the splendor of Heaven and the degree of seriousness we have for our task through every possible means.

I've yet to walk into a bridal shop and see ripped jeans and screen-printed T-shirts being worn by the sales staff. They are dressed quite nicely for many reasons. The people working in the bridal shop don't expect the brides-to-be to come into the store dressed as professionally as the sales staff are. The staff working there doesn't judge people for coming to the store in their street clothes because they know they are there to shop for a dress that will make them look their best on their wedding day.

Conversely, the brides-to-be that come to the store would feel the workers there didn't know anything about preparing a bride to look amazing for their "big day" if the staff were dressed casually in everyday street wear. In fact, they may even assume that the casually-dressed person didn't work at the shop and was also a customer. However, when the sales staff is dressed professionally, they project an image that instills confidence in the customer. The way the staff dresses also affects the staff member themselves as their professional attire puts them in the mindset to act professionally and take seriously the task of making women look and feel like royalty.

---

1. Ephesians 5:25-27

So, when leaders of the church dress their best and become conscious of the effect enclothed cognition has on them, it can positively affect the way we honor God in our leadership, the way we serve people, and the way we live out the sacredness of our calling. Conversely, dressing down all the time has been shown to lead to "relaxed manners, relaxed morals, and relaxed productivity."[1] We can outwardly dress down to alleviate the perception of being judgmental, yet inwardly still be judgmental.

Wearing culturally-relevant clothing does nothing to eliminate the perception or the reality of judgmentalism. In fact, I've personally seen church and ministry leaders who dress in the latest styles of the culture passing judgment on people who didn't (including other ministers). The same could also be said for leaders who dress professionally and pass judgment on those who are not. Ministers can choose to dress professionally or casually, but unless our hearts are enclothed with righteousness, the naked truth is that church leaders *will be* judgmental as the world perceives us to be—towards unbelievers, believers, and other church leaders alike. Once when Jesus was speaking to church and ministry leaders he said,

> You Pharisees and teachers are in for trouble! You're nothing but show-offs. You're like tombs that have been whitewashed. On the outside they are beautiful, but inside they are full of bones and filth. That's what you are like. Outside you look good, but inside you are evil and only pretend to be good.[2]

---

1. Karen E. Klein, "Dressed for Excess." Bloomberg.com. Bloomberg, January 8, 2001.

2. Matthew 23:27-28 (CEV)

Clothing Layer #3: OUTER LAYER

Jennifer Fulwiler authored an article for the *National Catholic Register* called "Why Don't We Dress Up Anymore?" One day while she had been in the airport, she noticed how carelessly dressed people were as they boarded the airplane. She recalled a black-and-white photo she'd recently seen of her grandparents getting onto an airplane back in the 1940's. Because air travel had been such a privilege at that time, people dressed accordingly, wearing suits/ties and dresses.

Fulwiler compared going to church to air travel now—it's no longer a big deal because people have a diminished sense of respect before God. If, however, the Queen of England was to invite them to Buckingham Palace they wouldn't be so casual with their choice of clothing. Shouldn't the minister have the same respect for the occasion to meet with God at his house—the church—and dress appropriately for it? And aren't we ourselves the temple of the Holy Spirit where Christ dwells?

Ministers (as well as all believers in Christ) are representatives of the Kingdom of God. We aren't the message, but rather the messengers. The Church isn't a corporation in competition with "The World, Inc." While dressing down doesn't make the Truth any more relatable than a dressing up makes the Truth respectable, how a minister chooses to dress says a lot about the level of respect they have for the message being presented.

When you factor in the effect that enclothed cognition has on the minister, choosing a comfortable, more casual style of dress has the effect of causing the minister to act more like a representative of the adopted values of culture rather than acting as a representative of the adopted values of God's Kingdom. Constance M. Cherry, author of *Worship Architect: A Blueprint for Designing Culturally Relevant and Biblically Faithful Services* said,

> Many young people and boomers judge the value of worship service based on personal satisfaction. If I get to wear flip-flops to Wal-Mart,

then I get to wear flip-flops to church. If I get to carry coffee to work, I get to carry coffee to church. They're being told that come as you are means that God wants you to be comfortable.

This is the ideology that the world has influenced the Church and its leaders to also adopt. In an effort to cater to the comfort-levels of those who don't regularly attend church, some ministers have mindlessly adopted this ideology to make *themselves* more comfortable. They succumb to the business-minded "the customer is always right" way of thinking. Consequently, they neglect to think about how clothing choices both *reflect* and *affect* their own respect for the Truth they represent.

There's a trade-off for making ourselves more comfortable by dressing like those in our culture. While we might feel like we're being more effective in convincing our audience to view us as being less judgmental and "one of them," we may become less effective in our leadership as our mental processes are affected by what we wear. Whether church leaders choose to dress trendy or traditional, we must be aware of the effects that enclothed cognition has on us. We, too, can become prideful and judgmental in comparing our clothes to what others are wearing. Satan did this when he was clothed in splendor.

Argument #2: *"I want our church/ministry to be thought of as RELEVANT in today's culture."*

In April of 2018, Mark Zuckerberg, Founder and Chief Executive Officer of *Facebook*, appeared before Congress. He had to give an account for how the company *Cambridge Analytica* was able to obtain and share the personal data of some ninety million Facebook users with third parties interested in using the data for campaign election purposes. If Facebook were a country, Zuckerberg would be the president over two-and-a-half-billion monthly active users worldwide. The congresspeople who questioned him only governed a population of 331 million citizens living in the United States. Zuckerberg's billion-dollar net-worth was greater than the *combined* net-worth of the congresspeople in the room who were questioning him.

While these powerful congresspeople wear business suits and professional attire to work every day, Zuckerberg normally wears a simple gray T-shirt and blue jeans. But during his testimony before Congress, he uncharacteristically wore a navy-colored suit and a bright blue tie.

It seems that most of today's elite Silicon Valley executives aren't wearing the iconic power suit or business-appropriate attire as a symbol of their position in their respective companies. Most are wearing the style of clothing that the average person on the street is wearing. T-shirts, sneakers, jeans, polo shirts, bomber jackets, and sweaters are all standard fare for them. The only difference seems to be that their clothing comes from high-end fashion designers.

Rather than a style of clothing being used to differentiate those of importance and status from those working for them, designer brands and the price paid for them are the differentiators. Take these for example: Jack Dorsey, CEO at both *Twitter* and *Square*, likes to wear Rick Owens brand sneakers that cost almost $1,000 a pair. Evan Spiegel, the CEO of *Snap* (the company that provides Snap Chat) likes to wear James Perse brand V-neck T-shirts that cost $60 (Zuckerberg's T's are from an Italian designer and cost only $49).

Why the change in clothing style for people in their positions?

Mark Dent suggests in an article he wrote which appeared in *Vox* "How the Power Suit Lost Its Power" that people nowadays seem to wear a suit when they are either in trouble or are not the person in control—as Zuckerberg was when he testified before Congress. Historically, the suit has been associated with projecting elegance and displaying status.

In the days when the workplace had been dominated by men, the upper-class CEO wore a suit. The middle-class employee wore a suit. Everyone wore a suit because the middle-class worker took pride in their work and wanted to be seen as being just as important as the CEO. Wearing a suit indicated that the individual wearing it was at the top of their profession. They were a person with authority. The middle-class worker wanted to project themselves in this light too, so they also wore a suit. Everyone dressed up because everyone wanted to present themselves to others wearing their best. (Nowadays we're more conscious of presenting our best to others on social media platforms than we are in person.)

Today, however, men don't primarily wear suits to work. In fact, JPMorgan downgraded its corporate dress code in 2016 to business casual. And just last year, Goldman Sachs did away with their requirement for suits to be worn in their company. Dent suggests that wearing a suit today now indicates just the opposite of what it used to mean. He says modern-day executives who are the ones *in* control, and not *under* it, possess an attitude that they can wear whatever they want. Deirdre Clemente, author of *Dress Casual: How College Students Redefined American Style*, writes, "There's a class element to it. To say 'I don't have to wear a suit' you have to be of a certain socio-economic class." This could be one reason why so many of today's corporate leaders aren't wearing business attire that has commonly been associated with their role. Today, only people who are under someone else's control are told what to wear or expected to wear certain clothing. Many middle-class workers can't simply choose what they want to wear to work.

Clothing Layer #3: OUTER LAYER

[Re]Organized Religion

While the mission of our churches and ministries is to build the Kingdom of God and not our own empires, the organizational structure and day-to-day operations of our ministries mirror that of businesses and corporations. (I will go into this in more depth in chapter 3.) Many of our churches and ministries use the same psychological tactics that businesses do regarding how we engage our audience. We use personality inventories to maximize the interactions and work environment of our staff. The same performance metrics as businesses are even used to evaluate the effectiveness of our churches and ministries.

As such, it makes sense that many pastors and ministry leaders are adopting the same attitude toward clothing styles that contemporary corporate CEO's have. In our fast-paced culture, perhaps it's our way of sending the message to the world that we're relevant and on the cutting-edge of our industry. If these corporate leaders who control large companies and manage employees, satisfy customers, and oversee large budgets aren't dressing like the professionals that they are, then church leaders might think people will perceive us as being both irrelevant *and* out of touch with today's culture. If the leader is thought to be irrelevant and out of touch, then the church or ministry we lead might also be thought to be irrelevant and out of touch.

I personally feel that church and ministry leaders who think and act this way when it comes to the issue of relevance have a confidence problem. There is a tendency for us to examine those whom either we ourselves or our society determines to be successful and emulate them. We look at what these successful businessmen and women do in their organizations, what they wear, etc., and copy them, thinking that both we and our ministries will also be perceived as up-to-date and successful (I'll refer you back to chapter one to explore the Survivor bias and Collins' *Good to Great* deception). We want to feel as though we're as relevant as those who are successful. The confidence to be different is what we're lacking.

Moreover, if we're to be truthful, church and ministry leaders may be trying to help God out by dressing less professionally. He does seem to have an image problem when the world looks at him and his Church you know. He hasn't authored a new book in well over two thousand years, or even updated his first one. Many of his teachings appear to be outdated in our progressive society. His laws, standards, and expectations haven't changed to reflect the will of the people like the laws of our country have. No wonder people just don't like God! He struggles with maintaining relevancy in our culture; church and ministry leaders must take up the slack and help God and his Church to become likeable and be viewed as relevant by today's standards, right? The Church seems to be moving in the direction of making Jesus *liked* and producing followers of our churches and ministers rather than making Jesus *Lord* and producing disciples that will be followers of Christ.

Psychological Layers of Clothing

What I find ironic is that five months after Mark Zuckerberg left his jeans and T-shirt in the dresser drawer and retrieved his suit from storage to make himself appear reputable before Congress, Sheryl Sandberg, the Chief Operations Officer of Facebook, also gave her testimony before Congress. Unlike Zuckerberg, however, she wore what she wears to work every day: a business-appropriate outfit. Both Zuckerberg and Sandberg are billionaires, and both are at the top of the game at Facebook. But, Zuckerberg dresses for work as if he's going *to* class, while Sandberg dresses for work *with* class.

Writing for *Women.com*, Laura Wagner states in her article "What Sheryl Sandberg Wears to Work" that Sandberg's clothing is a part of her authority and respect, which makes her ability to do her job exponentially greater. Sandberg has been quoted saying, "Being confident and believing in your own self-worth is necessary to achieving your potential." Confidence is created in-part by the caliber of clothing that's worn. While some leaders may argue that they consciously feel more confident when they're wearing more modern, casual clothes like everyone else, subconsciously they aren't.

The difference between Zuckerberg and Sandberg and the effect their clothing had on them is clear when you compare their two testimonies before Congress. The level of confidence that each had was different when they were in the room with Congress. Because Zuckerberg wasn't in his usual "unprofessional" attire, he was *subconsciously* uncomfortable and out of character while wearing a suit. Before he even answered the first question his subconscious was telling him that he wasn't confident and that he wasn't in control, even though the suit likely had positive benefits on him. However, the effect that enclothed cognition has had on Zuckerberg each day he wears his gray T-shirt and jeans is the exact opposite of what Sandberg's business-appropriate clothing tells her every day.

Subconsciously, Zuckerberg was like an irresponsible teenager having to stand before authoritative grownups. These members of Congress were already saturated with the effects that enclothed cognition has had on them. They've been wearing professional clothing every day and for many years. Zuckerberg projected himself both visibly and verbally as someone who wasn't in control of his organization. There were some twenty-nine questions he couldn't supply an answer for and had to defer the questions so that he could find out and report back to them.

Sandberg, on the other hand, walked into the congressional chamber with authority and confidence equal to that of the members of Congress who were in the room. The effect that enclothed cognition has had on her subconscious over time as she has dressed professionally for work every day had her project herself both visibly and verbally as a leader who was confident, responsible, and able to get something done about the situation. Unlike Zuckerberg, she deferred only four questions.

Zuckerberg's jeans and T-shirt had been deceitfully communicating to him. While he might have told himself that his clothing style (which ran contrary to one who has historically led from his position of power) portrayed him as one who was in charge, his clothes had been conveying a different message to his subconscious.

Basketball Coaches Wear Suits; Baseball Coaches Wear Jerseys

When we as ministry leaders worry more about our clothes portraying an image of relevance to the masses than portraying an image of responsibility to the Master, we fail as leaders. This is the heart of the matter. The clothing that church leaders choose to wear may be more beneficial to us when we wear them than they are to a skeptical audience. Clothes that embody leadership qualities help to instill more confidence and authority as we portray the relevance of both the gospel and the Church for today's world. While many church leaders have devoted a lot of time to leading people within our ministries, we ourselves have become the followers of those within our culture.

Leaders who think they must dress a certain way so that an unbelieving world will view the gospel as being relevant aren't leading. Rather, they're following the lead of a fickle crowd with varying and changing ideas about what's relevant. This kind of "leadership" is based upon a fear response to what people may think of the leader.

Clothing Layer #3: OUTER LAYER

We *must* put our faith in God and believe that he alone still has the power to draw people to him;[1] not the relevance of our clothing. God's Word, when it is spoken in the right season, is more relevant to people than if leaders are wearing what's trending this season. God's Church will have no problem establishing relevance if its leaders are effectively meeting people where they are and being/communicating God's message in a way that makes God the runway model—not the leader.

Basketball coaches aren't concerned that if they dress professionally players will think they don't understand the game and won't be able to lead the team to championship victory. In fact, dressing professionally may have the effect of enclothed cognition on the coach and instill in the players a sense of confidence in their coach's abilities. The coaches are convinced that they know how to lead the team to victory even if they aren't dressed in athletic attire themselves. Even if the coach has doubts about the team's ability to win against a stronger seated rival, or their own ability to coach their team to a victory, they can give off an air of confidence to both themselves and to their team by the way they're dressed to lead the team.

If the basketball coach were to dress like the players and act like a water boy following the team around, the team would not take the coach seriously. Neither would they have any confidence in the coach's ability to lead them. Church and ministry leaders are the coaches of God's team. People are looking to see what kind of leader the coach is before they decide to join the team; it's the coach who bears the responsibility of leading the team to victory.

We all want to be on a winning team and not just on a team where the coach wears a cool new jersey just like the players, even though people may want them to because it makes them look as if they can play the game. But people need coaches to

---

1. "The only way people come to me is by the Father who sent me—he pulls on their hearts to embrace me" John 6:44 (TPT).

Soliloquy № 7

be leaders. They may want the coach to look like a player, but if the coach can't lead the team to victory, they don't want to join the team. A.D. Sertillanges, in his book *The Intellectual Life,* said it this way:

> The only really powerful and really compelling force is strong conviction joined to a character which offers guarantees to poor humanity. The very people who require you to court their favour despise a flatterer and surrender to a master. If you are of this world, this world will love you because you are its own; but its silent disdain will be the measure of your fall.

The *armoire* was originally used to store weapons before it gradually became a place to store clothing. "Strong Conviction" and the "Character of Christ" are weapons that need to be on hand in our armoire of leadership. Clothes that meet the fashion approval of those who need for us to be leaders should not be in our arsenal of weaponry. Our goal is to provide people with Godly leadership and to "Taste and see that the Lord is good;"[1] not attempt to keep up with the latest fashion trends and get them to like us because of our taste in clothing.

If the standard by which ministers select their clothing is the trends of current culture, it causes a minister to spend a lot of effort studying the clothing trends of culture to make a statement to skeptical listeners. While the statement a minister may wish to make through their clothing is, "My clothing is relevant, just like the Truth that's found in the gospel message that I preach," the message to the observer can get crossed in translation to be interpreted as, "The Truth that is found in the gospel message that I preach is relative, just like the changing fashion trends that I wear."

---

1. Psalm 34:8

Ministers can inadvertently diminish the importance of the theological profession by de-emphasizing the role that clothing plays in regards to professionalism. It's an important psychological factor that influences both the minister and those being ministered to. Clothes can help the minister to take their ministry to people more seriously, and help those whom we minister to take us and the gospel more seriously.

It seems as if ministers who dress less than professional have adopted the cultural mindset that anything that must be upgraded has to be more valuable. It's as if our clothing has become a type of technology that's always needing to be updated. Things aren't upgraded to stay relevant with the times. Rather, updates to things are a commercial tactic used to *create* a sense of irrelevance. This is what drives our modern economic engine. Earlier versions of things lose value over time as people begin to devalue them in favor of the upgraded version.

This subconscious programming requires ministers looking to maintain the appearance of being culturally relevant through their clothing to submit to a type of *hedonic adaptation*[1] to the constantly shifting values of cultural relevance in terms of what must be worn to be perceived as being culturally relevant. Clothes that look professional, however, have a timeless way of maintaining the look of professionalism. Nassim Nicholas Taleb encapsulates this argument in his book *Antifragile: Things That Gain from Disorder*:

---

1. Hedonic adaptation is the general tendency for people to return to a preset level of happiness in spite of the ups and downs that life presents them with. In this context, we're never satisfied wearing the latest fashion trends. When we wear what's trending, we may experience happiness knowing that our clothing is relevant, but as soon as the trend changes, we're unhappy with our now irrelevant clothing and seek to acquire what is now in style. This process merely has us repeatedly trying to return to the same level of happiness we once had in wearing our previous clothing.

But it looks as though we don't incur the same treadmilling techno-dissatisfaction with classical art, older furniture—whatever we do not put in the category of the technological. You may have an oil painting and a flat-screen television set inhabiting the same room of your house. The oil painting is an imitation of a classic Flemish scene made close to a century ago, with the dark ominous skies of Flanders, majestic trees, and an uninspiring but calmative rural scene. I am quite certain that you are not eager to upgrade the oil painting but that soon your flat-screen TV set will be donated to the local chapter of some kidney foundation.

If clothing is going to function much like technology does and continually need to be upgraded to sustain relevancy (like Adam and Eve's fig leaves would have needed), the minister can never be satisfied with what's in their closet and will constantly feel as though they're being judged based on whether or not their clothing is up-to-date. If the minister's theology is up-to-date, and the power of the Spirit of God is flowing through them because they've been clothed in prayer, it wouldn't matter if they were wearing camel's hair like John the Baptist did. People will respond to the message if its timeless truths are presented with power. The relevance of the messenger's clothing becomes irrelevant. God's Word doesn't struggle with maintaining relevance.

Ministers need to take the theological profession seriously. When we do, we'll concern ourselves more with representing vocational ministry with the same (if not more) degree of professionalism that doctors and lawyers do in their professions. There's a lot more at stake in eternal matters than in temporal matters. In relating the Truth of the gospel to people and applying it to their lives today, the Spirit will draw them to the Truth, and the minister won't have to feel as though their clothing has to.

Argument #3: *"I want our church/ministry to be thought of as being RELATABLE by the people of today's culture."*

Some church leaders might suggest that dressing more like culture and less like clergy is a psychological tactic to make both themselves and their ministry appear more relatable to everyone—especially those who are skeptical of the church. This could have the effect of making the gospel appear more relatable. If the minister is dressed in a relatable and relevant way, then the gospel they preach must also be relatable and relevant.

I think this is merely a specious argument made up by church leaders who are more concerned about filling the seating capacity of their auditoriums than they are with the sending capacity that their ministry has. It is *quality* disciples that attend our churches who will take the message of Christ out into their circles of influence. If we were to push this ideology of "Come all into the church and be made disciples" further, we would find that those attending this type of church probably aren't fulfilling the Great Commission. They aren't the ones going out of the church to relay the message of the gospel to those around them and making disciples *themselves*. Instead, they're relegating that job to the church and its leaders. Besides, our churches only keep count of the number of salvations that happen inside the church on weekends, which sends the message that salvations outside the church on weekdays don't "count."

Without the benefit of disciples having already cultivated a relationship with those who need a relationship with God, the gospel could very well be considered unrelatable to the world. This could factor into the mentality that church leaders have in feeling as though they must be the ones who try to make the gospel appear more relatable through their clothing choices. The minister may be trying to make the church appear relatable in the absence of believers going out to build relationships with people who haven't been exposed to the church, the gospel message, or a genuine disciple. This, again, is deceitful communication that must be avoided. Why attempt to communicate to the world that both we and the gospel are relatable if we aren't going out into the world to build relationships with people and relate the gospel to them there?

We want to believe it shouldn't matter what type of clothing a leader chooses to wear if we're getting the job done. The camel hair clothing that John wore was quite a few notches below the priestly garments that the leaders in the Old Testament wore. It shouldn't matter if the church leader dressed professionally like basketball coaches do, or if we wore the same jersey that players wear like baseball coaches do.

Think about this: when a church or ministry leader stands in front of unbelievers, some would argue that to make the gospel message relatable to them, the minister needs to dress in a manner that unbelievers can relate to. Yet, when the minister stands behind a corpse lying in a casket in front of unbelievers, who are more aware at that moment that the certainty of death will come to them one day, somehow the minister feels it necessary to dress professionally for the occasion. I've yet to see a minister dress down as they conducted a funeral and ministered to people who may be at the most receptive point of receiving the gospel message that they'll ever be.

Why is this?

What's the thought process of the minister when it comes to choosing to wear culturally-relevant clothing to present the gospel on a Sunday morning to a mixed crowd of those who believe and those who have never heard the gospel, but dressing professionally to present the gospel at a funeral service to the same type of audience? At the Sunday service, the

Clothing Layer #3: OUTER LAYER

minister wants to feel as though their clothing is communicating to people that the gospel is relatable and that the minister is relatable also. At the funeral service, the minister wants to show respect for the solemnness of the occasion and to communicate that the gospel is an authority people can lean on as an anchor for their lives. The minister wants to communicate that they are an official representative of God's Church and they can lead those who are grieving the loss of life through this challenging time.

In both environments, what people are inwardly searching for is someone who will deliver Truth (which is the gospel) that will help them navigate through the uncertainties of life. God's Truth doesn't need help proving its trustworthiness. Truth only needs a spokesperson. The real question is, "To what degree does the messenger of the gospel respect the Truth?" When there's a diminished respect for the Truth inwardly, there most certainly will be a diminished respect for the Truth outwardly.

There may be something to the idea that leaders who dress in a more culturally-relevant and casual manner have the effect of making both themselves and the gospel appear more relatable to people. But if the message of the gospel depends on the clothing of the messenger to help the listener feel that it's relatable, then perhaps ministry leaders should realize that the members who sit in the church auditorium—the very ones that God has ordained to make the gospel relatable—are already dressed for the occasion every day!

Believers have been empowered to make the gospel message relatable through the established relationships they already have with the people they would invite to their church. Their friends and co-workers see them either dressed for work or dressed casually every day. However, church members just aren't relating the gospel in their relationships because of how they feel it will make them look. Believers would rather the responsibility be given to church leaders than to take the responsibility for making disciples themselves.

To that end, if church leaders have to resort to wearing clothing that makes new listeners feel that the gospel message is relatable, what kind of disciples would we actually be making when these same people find out that the gospel is actually offensive to a lifestyle of theological comfort, self-centeredness, and personal gratification? The answer is to continue the charade and clothe the gospel message—which is unrelatable to a human-centered lifestyle—with a different truth that's more relatable!

It boils down to this: Are church leaders more concerned about what people think of the gospel message or what Christ thinks of the gospel messenger? Christ takes more offense with church leaders who resort to giving *massages* from the pulpit to cause people to feel good about the gospel rather than *messages* from the cross to cause people to have a genuine and life-changing encounter with God.

***

In her book *You're Not Listening: What You're Missing and Why It Matters*, Kate Murphy talked about a famous qualitative research moderator named Naomi Henderson. In her job as a focus group moderator for almost fifty years, Naomi has moderated focus groups that have been responsible for giving feedback that established the looks and slogans of brands we buy and use today. These include the logo for American Express, the infamous Aunt Jemima, and Kentucky Fried Chicken's slogan "We Do Chicken Right!"

So, when Bill Clinton ran for President of the United States for the first time, Naomi was sought out to moderate focus groups and inform his campaign as to what voters thought about him. This information would be used to shape his image and provide him with the best chance of being elected. She discovered from listening to the focus groups that voters didn't like that he played up his Southern accent. "Here Clinton was a Rhodes Scholar, attended an Ivy League school, and he was the governor or Arkansas, and the focus groups wanted to know what part of that made him want to pretend to sound like a country guy who chews straw and drinks beer and drives a pickup truck," Naomi recalled as Murphy was interviewing her. "The people in the groups said, 'We don't need someone we can relate to, we'd rather have someone we can look up to.'"

CLOTHES-MINDED THINKERS

In addition to the three social character types of *tradition-directed*, *inner-directed*, and *outer-directed* that Riesman identified, towards the end of his book he offered a fourth type we should be striving for: *the autonomous*. He said that this social character type is embodied by "those who on the whole are capable of conforming to the behavioral norms of their society...but who are free to choose whether to conform or not."

What makes this the character type that church leaders should be striving toward is that those who can belong to this classification have the ability to understand the three other character types—see things from their perspectives—and independently choose when and if they should either comply with these other types or break from their viewpoint. Ministry leaders who are of the autonomous type have the vantage point of being missional and having, as Riesman puts it, "clear cut, internalized goals" that are individually chosen.

Autonomous character types become confident to the point that their "goals, and the drive towards them, are rational and non-authoritarian and not compulsive...maintaining the right of private judgment," says Riesman. To be an autonomous type of ministry leader, we would have to focus more on what we want or need our clothing to say *to* us and focus less upon what we want or need our clothing to say *about* us, to those we minister to, or to other church leaders.

Soliloquy № 7

Our clothing does say something about us to others. Did you ever stop to think that we as leaders may not be sending the message we want to convey when we wear clothes that aren't professional? What others think about us based on the clothes we wear can be quite different from what we want others to believe about us. When wearing ripped jeans and a bomber jacket, we may *want* to communicate to others that we're professionals who are confident and authoritative. But those who view us may interpret our choice of clothing as an attempt to hold on to our youth. This interpretation can cause people not to view us as professionals or not to view us as the person who is in charge.

Where's Superman When You Need Him?

The popular comic series *Superman* made its debut in 1938. Clark Kent, the main character, was from another planet. He had to keep his superpowers and the identity of his alter ego (Superman) hidden to protect those he loved from his enemies. As the story of Superman was developed when the daily clothing worn by men was a suit, Clark disguised himself by wearing a suit that draped loosely over his muscular physique. He wore a pair of glasses and parted his hair on the right.

Whenever there was a crisis and humanity needed his help, Clark found a phone booth to remove his disguise and became Superman. The clothing that everyone came to associate with Superman was a red and blue bodysuit with a long red cape and a large "S" on the chest. Unlike Clark, Superman didn't wear glasses and his hair was parted on the left. When Clark wore the same clothes as everyone else, no one expected that he could do anything about the crisis, even though, unknown to them, he *was* Superman. What's more, they never suspected that Clark Kent and Superman were the same person. It's amazing the power that his every-day appearance had on the way people perceived him.

When people encounter the difficulties of life, they need to be able to identify the leaders of the church as people that can help them in their time of need. If I were in serious legal trouble or had a child who had a life-threatening medical emergency, I wouldn't be looking for a lawyer or a doctor who looked "relevant" and wore skinny jeans, a hoodie, and red hi-top Converse shoes. Rather, I would be looking for someone who presented themselves as though they took their job seriously and were a professional in their field.

Our clothing professes something to us as well as to others. Ministers have something to profess to people who have broken God's law and need Jesus, the merciful judge. They're dying in their sins and need Jesus to be the healer of their souls. Ministers are professionals. We must consider whether or not the way we dress conveys that to those who encounter us.

Then there are messages our clothes may never communicate. To do so, the ideographic language of clothing would need to be redefined, and everyone in the world would have to agree to the new interpretation. For example, we can desire for the style of clothing that has the appearance of being (or actually *is*) "worn out" to communicate we're professionals and the leader of our organization. But until there's a global acceptance of that idea, and you see world political leaders from Tokyo on television wearing that style of clothing instead of a suit,[1] our "worn-out" clothing will never send that message. Michael Slepian, one of the authors of a study on formal clothing and professor of psychology at Columbia Business School said, "It takes a long time for symbols and our agreed interpretations

---

[1]. There is a street in Mayfair, central London, where bespoke men's suits have been made for the rich and wealthy since the seventeenth century. That street is named "Savile Row." Interestingly, the Japanese word for suit—"Sabiro"—comes from the phonetic pronunciation of that street.

of those symbols to change, and I wouldn't expect the suit as a symbol of power to be leaving us anytime soon."

Your Clothes Are "Lying" All Around You

Avoiding dishonest speech and perverse words as Solomon warns in Proverbs 4:24 can apply to the clothing we as ministers choose to wear. The *Random House Unabridged Dictionary* defines the word perverse as "willfully determined or disposed to go counter to what is expected or desired." If we're aware that our clothing embodies language and is influencing us through enclothed cognition, we should be more mindful to *not* wear clothes that send messages to our subconscious that will cause us to think, behave, and act in a manner that's not consistent with the level of professionalism that our responsibilities and positions of leadership in ministry demand.

Additionally, for church leaders to dress down, intending to lead people to believe that we and the gospel are relatable but then never taking the time to build relationships with those we're attempting to convince of our relatability, it technically makes us dishonest leaders as the language of our clothing is dishonest and perverse.

Are you a ministry leader that's relaxed in your responsibility of building the Kingdom of God? If you aren't, why be dishonest with yourself by wearing clothes that don't help you to be at your best in building God's Kingdom? And why not let God's Word and the Holy Spirit do their job and demonstrate just how relevant *they* are to humanity's problems that have existed since the fall of man? We need to do our job and present ourselves as taking the job of ministering to people seriously, and we can use all the help we can get to do this to the best of our ability.

Leaders must be mindful of the fact that we're representatives of a Kingdom that's not of this world. We must look beyond what we may perceive to be the obstacles that prevent people from receiving the Truth of the gospel. If the enemy didn't use clothing as a potential obstacle, he would use something else. We show more concern for things that don't really matter:

- The style of our worship music more than the theology of the lyrics.
- The use of technology for engaging unbelievers in the congregation more than the use of pneumatology through signs, wonders, and miracles.
- The ambiance of our sanctuary and facilities more than the church being a house of prayer.[1]

If the enemy can get church leaders to continually spin the plates of aesthetic relevance, we can end up being substantively irrelevant and neglect what really matters.

Admonishment #2: Don't let your clothing communicate dishonestly to you and reduce your level of effectiveness, respect, and professionalism for the work God has appointed you to do for him. Before you ever step into your role as a leader, your clothing has had your subconscious step into the role of your style of clothing.

---

1. "When the Sabbath day came, we went outside the gates of the city to the nearby river, for there appeared to be **a house of prayer and worship** there. Sitting on the riverbank we struck up a conversation with some of the women who had gathered there. One of them was Lydia, a businesswoman from the city of Thyatira who was a dealer of exquisite purple cloth and a Jewish convert. While Paul shared the good news with her, God opened her heart to receive Paul's message. She devoted herself to the Lord, and we baptized her and her entire family" Acts 16:13-15 (TPT) [emphasis added].

Soliloquy № 7

Questions:

- When you look in the mirror, have you ever asked what messages your clothes are sending to you and not just to others?
- How did you come to choose the style of clothing you wear in your ministry?
- Are your clothing choices directed by tradition, personal preference, or have you conformed to the trends of the mainstream without stopping to think if the mainstream is flowing the wrong direction?
- Do you lack the confidence to dress your best and be viewed as a professional?
- If you were a doctor or a lawyer, how would dressing the way you do now in ministry impact your patients/clients, and how might the medical community or judges/other lawyers view you?
- If you are dressing for personal comfort, how is it that your comfort level takes priority over professionalism?

"Set your gaze on the path before you. With fixed purpose, looking straight ahead, ignore life's distractions."

Proverbs 4:25 (TPT)

THREE

ARCHITECTS OF THE ARCHETYPE:
Fixating on Purpose & the Swimmer's Body Illusion

"Trees: The REAL Cause of Forest Fires"

—Bennett Lear Fairorth,
Dear Jon: Letters to and
from a Former Teacher,
9-11-93 to 11-9-04

Soliloquy № 7

CONSTRUCTION PHASE #1:
FOUNDATION

PRUITT-IGOE

On September 2, 1945, surrender documents were signed by Japanese leaders on board the American battleship, the USS Missouri. The Second World War had come to an end. At this time, there were eight million US Allied military personnel waiting to come back to the United States from their overseas posts in Asia and Europe. "Operation Magic Carpet" got underway in December of 1945 to bring our troops home, and after fourteen months of relentless efforts, they finally arrived. But it was not the same country they left.

Before the war had begun, agriculture was one of the largest employers in the economy of our nation. As the war continued, more and more farm workers were drafted into military service. In addition, the factories that were producing everything to supply the war effort were paying higher wages, which caused many farm laborers to find jobs in the factories. Subsequently, a shortage of farm workers was created. This forced those who continued farming to become more efficient and more productive. Because farm equipment had to take the place of people, farm equipment manufacturers had to improve their tractors and their implements while making them more affordable to meet the demand.

Mechanized labor had eliminated the need for labor-intensive methods of farming. Fewer people were needed to plant, cultivate, and harvest a crop. One man could sit atop a tractor and do what used to take many hired hands to do. This especially impacted farming in the South, and a large migration to the North began. Farmers and laborers who could make a living at farming before the war began were no longer able to

Construction Phase #1: FOUNDATION

do so. As they began to migrate northward in search of work to provide for their families, they found themselves relocating to cities where factories were producing products to furnish the American home.

Five years after Captain Stuart S. Murray had taken command of the USS Missouri and assumed responsibility to prepare for the signing of the Japanese surrender, a Japanese-American by the name of Minoru Yamasaki had taken responsibility as the lead architect for the building of the Captain Wendell O. Pruitt Homes and the William L. Igoe Apartments. These urban renewal projects would be built on fifty-seven acres at the edge of downtown St. Louis in Missouri, and would come to be known as "Pruitt-Igoe."

The city planners of St. Louis had been anticipating an estimated population growth of about one million residents living within the city limits by 1970. But as thousands of farmers, laborers, and low-wage, unskilled workers arrived in St. Louis, the only place they could afford to live was in the slums of the city. The slums were affordable to these low-wage earners, but cheap has two meanings: *low cost* and *poor quality*. The slums were also dangerous and unsanitary.

Because the city boundaries of St. Louis were established in the nineteenth century, it was mandated that the borders of the city couldn't expand outward as other major cities were able to do. Therefore, city officials looked at accommodating the expanding population growth by growing upwards with planned housing developments. These developments were made possible by the American Housing Act of 1949, which provided the funding for the construction of public housing. The St. Louis Land Clearance and Redevelopment Authority would acquire and clear the slums and replace these dangerous and unsanitary dwellings with a public housing oasis containing 2,970 housing units. These would become home to some twelve-to-fifteen thousand tenants.

Soliloquy № 7

Yamasaki held the belief that design solutions and building architecture could change behavior in both positive and predictable ways. This idea had been embraced throughout the centuries by several other architects. In the 1400s, Italian architect Leon Battista Alberti held the belief that balanced classical forms of architectural structures would compel invading aggressors to exchange their instruments of warfare and become peaceful citizens. The famous American architect Frank Lloyd Wright believed architecture could abate corruption by turning US citizens back towards wholesome activity. Ebenezer Howard, a British author, posited that corporations could become more efficient if the workforce were to live in village-like garden communities. Charles-Édouard Jeanneret, a French architect born in Switzerland (who was known as Le Corbusier), made claims that his house design named the *Villa Savoye* would increase health and well-being to those who would live in it. (It ended up doing just the opposite to the inhabitants. Le Corbusier avoided court only because World War II began and the owners had to vacate it.)

Believing that architecture has the power to change people's behaviors in positive and predictable ways would later come to be known as *architectural determinism*. British planner Maurice Broady coined the term in a paper he published in 1966 entitled, "Social Theory in Architectural Design."

The basic premise of this theory is that by removing a person from their previous habitation and placing them in an environment that was, from an architectural standpoint, strategically planned to predict and determine the outcomes of their behavior, it would promote changes in how these people came to view themselves in light of their surroundings. Adherents to this view believed these environmental and structural enhancements would ultimately cause people's behavior to change.

The idea of architectural determinism was embraced to the point that architectural writer Adolph Behne was quoted as saying, "You can kill a man with a building just as easily as with an axe." His thought was that if one could kill a man with a building, then one could just as easily *change* a man with a building.

The complex which Yamasaki designed was a modernist approach that embodied architectural determinism. As Rowan Moore writes of Yamasaki's design in his article for *The Guardian*, "Pruitt-Igoe: Death of the American Dream":

> Yamasaki professed humanity, harmony and his opposition to prejudice, beliefs born out of his experiences as a put-upon Japanese American. He laid out Pruitt-Igoe according to the best principles of the modern movement: an orderly plan in which cars and pedestrians were separated, ample open space was provided between the blocks, and flats were oriented to catch daylight and views.

In 1955, when the complex began to open, tenants who had moved out of the slums and into the Pruitt-Igoe complex described it as "an oasis in the desert." They had come from abject poverty and had seemingly moved into another world where the homes were completely furnished, and everyone had their own bed.

Yamasaki had originally designed the complex as a mixed-rise cluster of buildings. The Public Housing Administration, however, balked at the cost of building his original design and insisted on a uniform tower height of eleven stories. Because of construction budget constraints imposed by the government who funded these public housing projects, corners were cut in the quality of construction and in the fixtures and furnishings that were installed. These began to immediately show after the first tenants took occupancy, but they didn't seem to bother anyone as they had just come out of much worse living conditions.

Soliloquy № 7

In 1957, the occupancy rate of the complex had been at ninety-one percent. But just over ten years after Pruitt-Igoe opened, the housing complex began to be criticized for its deteriorated condition, and the occupancy rate began to decline. Many factors brought about this decline, including a change in public policy in segregation law, low-cost mortgages for home ownership, and fiscal instability.

As the occupancy continued to decline, so did the behavior of the remaining occupants. Over ten thousand windows were broken, furnishings hurled from the roof, and copper wire had been stripped from the walls. Gerald Celente, founder of the Trends Research Institute, once said, "When people have nothing left to lose, and they have lost everything, they lose it." What was left of the "oasis in the desert" was just—well, a desert. Yamasaki himself would later say about the complex he designed: "I never thought people were that destructive. It's a job I wish I hadn't done."

On March 16, 1972, all remaining tenants were consolidated to eleven of the thirty-three buildings that had been constructed, and demolition of the vacant buildings began. Only eight hundred tenants remained in 1973—a fragment of the nearly fifteen thousand residents that once happily lived there. By 1977, Pruitt-Igoe was no more. It seemed that the metaphor had been reversed from "You can kill a man with a building just as easily as with an axe," to "A *man* can kill a building by himself just as easily as with a wrecking ball."

In the span of time equivalent to the length of one generation (about twenty years), the architectural design that was thought to be able to determine and change the behavior of people in positive and predictable ways ended up not being able to do so. The buildings were merely a temporary distraction that caused people—many who were desperately in need of something that would change their circumstances and their outlook on life—to only take a reprieve from their innate nature, leaving them unchanged in their behavior.

Construction Phase #1: FOUNDATION

Rowan Moore concluded, "The effects of architecture alone are rarely as significant as people think: it can certainly affect your sense of wellbeing for better or worse, and it can aid or it can hinder the larger forces that it serves." But there is something deeper that has to be addressed in the heart and soul of man if man is to change. It's not the place where we dwell that changes us, but rather it's what dwells within that place inside of us that makes a change in us.

THE SWIMMER'S BODY ILLUSION

The case of Pruitt-Igoe is an example of where people had fallen prey to a bias called the *Swimmer's Body Illusion*. Nassim Nicholas Taleb wrote in his book, *The Black Swan: The Impact of the Highly Improbable,* about a time he began to take notice of the physiology of various athletes. He was searching for some athletic activity in which he could involve himself. Runners, he said, tended to look emaciated. Bicycle riders had a lower body that seemed disproportionate to the top half of their bodies. Those who aggressively lifted weights appeared to compensate outwardly for some internal weakness and produced a body that was more or less a regression towards an age when hunter-gatherer societies required this type of physique for survival. Swimmers, however, seemed to possess elongated muscles that produced a body shape that appeared strong, elegant, and pleasing to the eye.

So, Taleb decided that he would start swimming twice a week at his area swimming pool in an attempt to create one of these types of bodies for himself. After some time of endeavoring at this activity, it dawned on him that swimmers may not obtain this type of perfect physique as a result of their dedicated efforts of swimming laps. Perhaps they were natural swimmers because they already *had* this type of physique.

Soliloquy № 7

It seems that the way that our bodies are designed plays an important role in determining the athletic activity for which we may be particularly "fit." This concept reaches beyond athleticism. Playing the piano or a stringed instrument doesn't *give* you the long fingers that can span the keyboard or fretboard to maneuver fluidly and produce beautiful music. People *with* long fingers play the piano or a stringed instrument with fluidity because they *have* long fingers.

Rolf Dobeli poses the question, "Does Harvard make you smarter?" in his book *The Art of Thinking Clearly*. He wondered if it's possible that smarter people go to Harvard rather than come out of it. Likewise, do products in the cosmetics, beauty care, and fashion industries make everyone as beautiful as the models that are used to advertise the products, or are the models selected to advertise these products because they're already beautiful people? Anytime we confuse what is being brought *to* the table with the outcomes we anticipate coming *from* the table we fall prey to the Swimmer's Body Illusion.

In the case of Pruitt-Igoe, the Swimmer's Body Illusion was the fixation that you could positively change a person's thought patterns and behaviors by removing them from their poverty-stricken slums (that produced negative thought patterns and delinquent behaviors) and house them in newly-constructed, fully furnished buildings. While outside forces can *influence* people's thoughts and behaviors, it takes inside forces to *change* them.

Since it's easier to change the outer world of people's environments than it is to change the inner world of people's minds, we often look for ways to manipulate the outer world and think it will help to change the inner one. Because of the way our minds operate, we look for identifiable patterns or causations we can correlate to achievable outcomes (like swimming laps to achieve a lean, muscular physique). Our tendency for trying to find connections and meaning between things in order to make sense of the world around us (*apophenia*[1]) often causes us to make mistakes in our correlations.

The Swimmer's Body Illusion can show up in our churches in a variety of ways—for example, in our worship services. In our present culture of modern worship songs, this cognitive bias can be observed when a few measures of a song have everyone singing out the word, "Whoa!" as the only lyric. The energy of the audience increases; people begin to sing out (perhaps because it is an easy word to sing), and apophenia leads us to believe that God's presence has intensified as indicated by the increased response of the worshippers.

Singing out the word "Whoa!" in unison and with volume isn't the key that unlocks the door to open us up to the presence of God. While it may cause everyone to sing out (and it may sound great in the song), it does more to create an emotional response in the singer than it does to extol the greatness of our God. As Barbara Kingsolver writes in her book, *Flight Behavior*, "Cars with flames painted on the hood might get more speeding tickets. Are the flames making the cars go fast? No. Certain things just go together. And when they do, they are correlated. It is the darling of all human errors to assume, without proper testing, that one is the cause of the other." This is an example of the Swimmer's Body Illusion.

The Discipleship Illusion

One of the most detrimental ways that the Swimmer's Body Illusion can affect the Church is in the area of discipleship. The fixation on the Swimmer's Body Illusion can cause disciple

---

1. *Apophenia:* The term was first used in 1958 by German psychiatrist Klaus Conrad in his book *Die beginnende Schizophrenie; Versuch einer Gestaltanalyse des Wahns* [*The Onset of Schizophrenia: An Attempt to Form an Analysis of Delusion*].

Soliloquy № 7

making to become an illusion as church leaders explore methods to fulfill the Great Commission. We know the mission that Jesus gave to believers was to make disciples.[1] This is the full-time job of the Church, and all activities must be centered on this one thing.

Got it.

Make disciples.

How do we make disciples? What does this involve? What's required of a disciple maker, and what's the responsibility of the one who is a disciple? How do we know whether we've made a disciple? This is where the Swimmer's Body Illusion can begin to affect the church leader and create a discipleship illusion. There are many activities—both personal and corporate—that are correlated with becoming a disciple, being a disciple, and making disciples. We can easily make the mistake of correlating these external activities with the means by which disciples are made. But these activities don't cause disciples to be made.

If we were to compare the church to the case of Pruitt-Igoe, church leaders could make the same mistake Yamasaki made in believing that architectural determinism could change people. We can mistakenly fall prey to the Swimmer's Body Illusion, thinking that the way to positively change the thinking patterns and subsequent behaviors of those who have been living in spiritual poverty is to simply get them to come to church, let them see people worshipping God, and have them listen to the preaching of the gospel. If we can accomplish that, we think we're engaged in disciple making. While it's good for unbelievers to go to church, their attendance doesn't make them into disciples. Neither does it make us disciple makers. Unbelievers may continue to faithfully attend church services, begin to participate in worship, and even say a prayer for salvation, but these things don't make someone a disciple.

---

1. Matthew 28:19

Construction Phase #1: FOUNDATION

Didn't the Pharisees watch people worship Jesus and hear him teach? Doesn't the Bible say that not everyone who calls him "Lord" will enter the Kingdom of Heaven?[1] Wasn't it the same crowd who welcomed Jesus to Jerusalem with palm branches and shouts of "Hosanna!" at the beginning of the week, that also shouted "Crucify him!" at the end of the week? The Swimmer's Body Illusion can trick us into thinking that correlated outward activities produce internal changes.

No. External factors are not the *cause* of internal changes. Swimming doesn't produce a swimmer's body. Living in Pruitt-Igoe didn't remove a poverty mentality. Going to the bank doesn't make you wealthy. And going to church doesn't make you a disciple. Rather, internal factors cause external changes. People whose physique is genetically predisposed to gliding through the water with force and speed become great swimmers in a pool (a Sumo wrestler will never develop a swimmer's body by swimming). Those who don't possess a poverty mentality won't destroy their environment but, rather, will work to find solutions to make it better. Work produces wealth that gets deposited in the bank. Individuals on a journey to discover who Jesus is will attend church.

Internal forces must be at work inside of an individual before outside forces can support them. We are spiritual beings, and it takes the Spirit of the living God to bring life to those who are spiritually dead in their sins. In a spiritual sense, we all have within us the capability of a "swimmer's body." But it has to first be brought to life by the Holy Spirit before the church or its activities can help in its development.

---

1. Matthew 7:21-23

Soliloquy № 7

CONSTRUCTION PHASE #2:
FRAMING

DISCIPLE BUILDING

Brad Borland, a former competitive bodybuilder and author of the book, *Bodybuilding Basic Training: The Absolute Beginner's Guide to Building Muscle*, identifies three different purposes a person may have when it comes to bodybuilding: aesthetics, strength, or power. As a Certified Strength and Conditioning Specialist for over twenty years with the National Strength and Conditioning Association, he has experience in helping people to achieve any of these three bodybuilding goals. No matter which of these three goals a person may attempt to achieve, it will require them to make some changes to their lifestyle.

They will need to adjust their schedule to make time to get to the gym, lift weights according to some training regimen under the supervision of a personal trainer, modify their diet, take supplementation, and form new lifestyle habits. The only way any of these modifications will work for a person is if there's a total abandonment to their former lifestyle (which perhaps consisted of sitting on the couch and eating fatty foods) and a total commitment to a dietary and training program of a personal trainer.

Borrowing from the idea of bodybuilding, when it comes to *disciple building*, Jesus indicated that the process for everyone who would follow him as a disciple begins with the requirement that they cease from pursuing their own selfish will for their lives and commit to submitting to his will for their lives.[1] Architectural determinism according to God is that *he* is the Divine Architect who has determined the design for what our

---

1. Mark 8:34

"temple" should look like, and we need to submit to his plans to make us into the image of his Son, Jesus. We must exchange our architectural blueprints for the life we're attempting to build for the plans he has established for us before he ever created the universe.

A church, with its people and programs, can create the environments and offer the support to assist with this process, but the individual willingly has to surrender their own will to God. We aren't supposed to build our lives according to the blueprints of our sinful nature but allow our blueprints to be completely altered so our lives can be transformed and built according to the perfect will of God's architectural plan for us.[1] His plan is that we ultimately look like Christ. In order for us to successfully be made into his disciples, our nature has to be completely remade.

Training for Aesthetics

Let's get back to the bodybuilding analogy and look at the three different goals of bodybuilding and apply them to disciple building. First, let's examine the goal of training for aesthetics — merely reshaping the physique so as to look good. Those with this goal want to have a body that has muscle definition, giving the appearance of being fit, healthy, and strong. They work out in order to reshape their bodies and are focused only on increasing the size of their muscles for aesthetic purposes — to *look* good.

To accomplish this goal, Borland says the ideal training routine will include lifting only sixty-five to eighty-five percent of the person's one-repetition maximum weight, increasing the number of repetitions of the exercise they're doing in each set, while taking a very brief rest period between sets. In this way,

---

1. Romans 12:2

they'll lift a lighter load more times with little rest between sets. This type of training will cause the muscle fibers to increase in volume and grow larger, thus making the muscles of the body grow larger and increase in size. Brad states, "If you are training for the sheer purpose to build muscle and reshape your physique, then you need to fatigue the muscle with moderate reps [repetitions], plenty of volume, and short rest periods. Your focus should be on the muscle working versus the load lifted."

There are many churches and church leaders—gyms and personal trainers if you will—who take an aesthetic approach to disciple building by having followers of Christ engage in a training process that causes them to outwardly *look* like a disciple of Christ. The training program for aesthetic disciple building involves faithfully attending church services and frequently participating in various programs and ministries of the church. This process of making disciples can lead church leaders to believe we are making and strengthening disciples when we are really only making people *look* like a disciple. People are in the gym (church) and have gone through the repetitive motions (programs) with the least resistance needed to become aesthetically fit. Aesthetic disciple building leads people to believe that they are a disciple of Christ because they *look* the part of a disciple, but in reality, they have taken the "path of least resistance" and are devoid of any strength or power.

While it's true that disciples should engage in church activities, true disciple building involves more than participating in activities that have a person repetitively and routinely attending services and participating in programs. Aesthetic disciple building essentially under-challenges a disciple's faith and the potential they have for becoming spiritually stronger. Many people will settle for this version of discipleship—looking like a disciple by attending all the things disciples of Christ attend, but never really developing the strength that true discipleship can develop or the power to fight in spiritual warfare.

Construction Phase #2: FRAMING

For church leaders attempting to train disciples with the goal of aesthetics in mind, their idea of disciple making is to increase the size of the church. If the church is the "body" of Christ, and church leaders function like personal trainers in a gym, the purpose of church growth in aesthetic disciple building is to focus on the size of the body of Christ, increasing it so that it looks good and appears strong. The more people who are coming to church services and attending church programs gives the appearance that disciples are being made into the image of Christ because the size of the body of Christ is increasing and it also looks strong. This is the Swimmer's Body Illusion working on the church leader's mind. This is the Church of Pruitt-Igoe.

You can't expect people to develop into the image of Christ by merely attending church services and participating in programs. This change can only take place when the genetics of the inner spirit-man are changed into a new creation that's pre-disposed to, and has the potential for, transforming disciples into the image of Christ.

Karl Vaters, author of *Small Church Essentials: Field-Tested Principles for Leading a Healthy Congregation of under 250*, once wrote in an article for *Christianity Today*, "The value of what God is doing in people's lives can't be accurately measured by how many sit in a weekend church service, or in a discipleship class." The church exists to be a place where lives can change and transform into the image of Christ through discipleship, but growing the size of the body of Christ only through church attendance and program participation doesn't produce disciples that have the strength to fight spiritual battles, overcome the enemy's obstacles, and live victorious lives.

Jesus called his disciples by saying to them, "Follow me."[1] This phrase is found twenty-one times in the New Testament, using two different Greek words. In the two accounts found in the Gospels, where Jesus calls some of the disciples to follow

---

1. Matthew 4:19

Soliloquy № 7

him so he could make them into fishers of men, both accounts use the Greek word *opiso* for "Follow me."[1] *Opiso* means literally "to get behind, come after, and to be at one's back." It is used to indicate a placement. In the other nineteen places that the phrase "follow me" is recorded, the Greek word *akoloutheo* is used. This word means "to follow someone as a disciple and imitate them as you accompany them."

There are many aesthetic disciples today who are following Jesus (*opiso*), but aren't following Jesus (*akoloutheo*). They may be where Jesus is geographically and associating with the activities that would identify them as one of Christ's disciples, but they aren't capable of doing what Jesus said his disciples would be able to do after he left. The reason for this is that they haven't begun to do the things Jesus did when he was on earth.

Training for Strength

The second bodybuilding goal Borland identifies is training for strength. Those who pursue this goal focus on being able to lift the maximum amount of weight to develop a high level of body strength. He says that those who train for strength are more interested in performance than they are in aesthetics. In their training routines they will lift between eighty-five to ninety percent of their one-repetition maximum weight max for two-to-six repetitions in each set, but with two-to-five minutes of rest in between. Simply stated, they lift heavier weights fewer times with more rest. While the muscles will grow in size as they do with aesthetic training, they will also be capable of enduring and overcoming resistance to their efforts.

Genuine disciples should not be led to believe by their disciple-making personal trainer/church leader that mere "lightweight" aesthetic discipleship training will make them into a

---

1. Matthew 4:19; Mark 1:17

stronger disciple of Christ. Guiding disciples into committing their lives to the will of Christ entails helping them to focus on strengthening their internal spirit-man. Disciple builders must place their focus on participating in the activities that Jesus did and daily apply themselves to shaping their own spirit-man into the image of *the* Spirit-Man.

Jesus grew in strength by getting away from the crowds and praying in solitude. He also fasted, studied the scriptures, fostered friendships with sinners, shared the Good News through preaching and teaching, and mentored a small group of young men. Church discipleship training programs designed to make aesthetic disciples don't typically have disciple builders engaged in these kinds of activities because more commitment is required of both the disciple builder and the disciple maker. And the deeper the level of commitment to Christ, the smaller the numbers of strong disciples that are being made tend to be. If growing in numerical size is the measure of your success, growing strong disciples may be disappointing.

Jesus grew in both external and internal disciplines. By exercising and strengthening the internal disciplines, such as through prayer, studying the scriptures, fasting, etc., he was empowered to exercise the external disciplines, such as teaching, mentoring, serving, etc. Both internal and external disciplines are needed. Engaging in the internal exercises of spiritual disciplines without external engagement leaves a disciple focused on only the first of the two great commandments: loving the Lord our God with all our heart, soul, mind, and strength.[1] Likewise, engaging in only outward disciplines has disciples operating under their own gifts and talents and focused on the second great commandment (loving their neighbor as they love themselves) without relying on the strength that can only be gained from exercising internal disciplines.

---

1. Mark 12:29-30

Soliloquy № 7

If a bodybuilder who was training for strength focused their training only internally by eating the right ratio of carbohydrates to protein, taking proper supplementation, and getting adequate rest, but didn't externally exercise their body by lifting weights, they wouldn't grow in strength. Neither would they grow stronger if they externally exercised the body by lifting weights without internally preparing their body to have the energy it needed to sustain and even increase the demands being placed upon it. Disciple building for strength requires a disciple to have a dual focus on both increasing their internal spiritual power as well as participating in external spiritual service.

Fully expecting to make strong disciples, disciple makers will often adopt a disciple-making ideology that either places more emphasis on an internal strength-training program, or one that places more emphasis on an external strength-training program. In reality, making disciples who possess the strength to inwardly fight spiritual battles as well as to outwardly impact the lives of those around them requires the focus be placed on *both* internal and external training in tandem.

Many churches adopt an ideology that promotes an external approach to disciple building as the first step in a disciple's faith journey following salvation. The church attempts to help the new disciple find a place to serve others and use their own strengths—their personalities, their experiences, their passions, and their natural/spiritual giftings—in order to grow and be strengthened in their spiritual lives. This approach does cause disciples to do more than merely attend services and programs (as in aesthetic disciple building) by adding some "weight" to their spiritual growth. However, this is an incomplete method for a disciple to follow to grow and gain spiritual strength.

When this one-sided external approach is taken, people end up "burning out" as they grow tired of carrying the burden of ministry under their own strength. They don't refresh their internal spirit-man by taking the time to rest in God's presence.

Construction Phase #2: FRAMING

When this is the approach that's taken, those using their outward strengths come to church and participate in the various avenues of ministry that will help the church accomplish its vision for missional effectiveness in their programs, but these disciples become "maxed out" and their strength is spent rather than built up.

That would be like a bodybuilder going to the gym to help the personal trainer or gym accomplish their business goals. Instead of focusing on teaching disciples to help accomplish the *church's* vision, we as disciple makers should be training disciples to accomplish God's vision for *their own lives* so that they can become disciples that look and function as Christ did. We must consider not only the way we train disciples to function within the church's ministries, but also in the way they function as disciples outside of the church's ministries.

The other one-sided ideology is to promote an internal approach to disciple building. This approach places the focus on strengthening the inward man by practicing a regiment of spiritual disciplines. Daily prayer and Bible reading, intentional prayer and fasting, studying scripture, memorizing and meditating on scripture, reflective worship—there are a variety of ways to grow strong in the internal dimension of our spiritual lives. Just as the external approach is an incomplete method of growing strong as a disciple when it becomes the sole focus of training, the internal approach is also an incomplete disciple building method for a disciple to grow and gain spiritual strength.

Internal faith is lifeless without external works.[1] There may be a large number of church leaders who think that they're making strong disciples because those under their leadership are faithfully practicing these internal disciplines. While this is true, it is only half-true. An organism grows when its cells grow and begin to multiply. However, a cell wall has two sides

---

1. James 2:17

to it: the interior wall and the exterior wall. The whole truth is that disciples are made strong when disciple building focuses on both interior strength training and exterior strength training. These two approaches are dependent upon one another. Exterior strength training must be coupled with interior strength training. Teaching people God's Word (external) requires studying God's Word (internal). Evangelizing the world with the gospel (external) requires prayer (internal). Serving the needs of others in an attempt to let God's love break through hardened hearts (external) requires fasting and prayer (internal).

Sometimes it seems as though some church leaders think they're making disciples simply because their ministries are increasing in size. To them, this must mean that those attending must also be growing into the image of Christ because—clearly—they must be doing something that's missionally-effective if they are attracting more people to their ministry.

There are other church leaders who seem to acknowledge that aesthetic disciple building, through corporate methods that attempt to mass produce disciples, isn't actually making disciples. Aesthetic disciple makers want to make disciples who will have the strength to function as Jesus spoke of and modeled, but a holistic approach to inward/outward strength training isn't taken.

Both aesthetic and half-strength disciples may follow Jesus around, but they aren't capable of doing what Jesus did or what he said that his disciples would be able to do. Church leaders are much closer to making the kind of disciple Jesus had in mind when they focus on both the internal and external growth of disciples simultaneously.

Even when we begin to address both the inward and outward strength that need developing in a more holistic manner, and we see more disciples being made (making disciples always multiplies the church, whereas making converts merely adds to it), there's still one more aspect of disciple building that needs to be addressed.

Construction Phase #2: FRAMING

Training for Power

The third goal that Borland identifies is training for power. The goal of this bodybuilding approach is to move a load of weight at a very high rate of speed. Unlike training for strength, which focuses on how much weight can be lifted, power training focuses on moving heavy weight quickly. Brad writes that training for power "is a compliment to pure strength training, in that strength training will provide stability and whole-body strength, while power will increase the rate of muscle fiber recruitment." What is unique about power training is that the weight and repetition can vary anywhere from ninety percent of an individual's one-rep maximum weight lifted only one to two times, to twenty to thirty percent of their one-rep maximum lifted up to five times. Training for power, in addition to strength training, is why boxers can quickly strike a blow to their opponents (speed) and knock them out because of the force applied (strength).

In terms of disciple building, the same importance needs to be placed on strengthening both one's inward love for God and one's outward love for people. But a third goal of speed is necessary, especially if *true* disciples take seriously the lost condition of humanity, the enormity of the number of people who are not in relationship with Christ as their Savior and Lord, and the uncertainty of time remaining before Christ returns. With believers having a mandate to make disciples until Christ returns, and time running out to fulfill that mandate, we need the element of speed woven into our disciple building.

Did you ever realize that in only about three-years', Jesus went from no one knowing who he was to—at one point— having a crowd of over five thousand men (excluding women and children) present for his ministry? In this short amount of time, Jesus managed to shake up the religious establishment and began a movement because of the demonstration of power that accompanied him. Luke 4:32 says that "His teaching amazed them because he spoke with power" (CEV). Not only did Jesus demonstrate power in his ministry to people, Luke 9:1-2, 6 says that "He called the twelve together and gave them power and authority over all demons and to cure diseases, and he sent them out to proclaim the kingdom of God and to heal... And they departed and went through the villages, preaching the gospel and healing everywhere."

FOLLOW THE LEADER

Throughout the Gospels, we find Jesus describing the outcomes and indicators of a person who is a disciple. Some of these things include loving one another[1] and continuing in his Word.[2] These are things that ALL disciples—no matter how new or how old, both in biological and "discipilogical" age—should be doing. All disciples should communicate with Christ in prayer, read the Bible, faithfully attend church, and worship God. As disciples continue to follow Christ and grow in their discipleship efforts, they'll begin to produce fruit.[3] The fruit of discipleship includes making more disciples and displaying the spiritual evidences of love, joy, peace, patience, etc. as found in Galatians 5:22.

There does, however, seem to be a difference between what we identify as a disciple of Jesus Christ today and what Jesus would have identified as a disciple during his earthly ministry. In the first five chapters of Mark's Gospel account, we read that Jesus called the disciples to follow him, and they observed him as he taught and performed miraculous signs. During this time, the disciples were not the ones operating in power. All we read

---

1. John 13:35
2. John 8:31
3. John 15:8

Construction Phase #2: FRAMING

of them is that they're simply following Jesus, listening to his teaching, and watching as he performed miracles.

Some church leaders today believe that this is all there is to making disciples. These leaders would settle for making aesthetic disciples who are present when biblical teaching is presented and allow only "qualified" individuals to pray for the sick and see the miraculous done in peoples' lives. Many church leaders are lulled by the enemy into believing that disciple making mainly consists of calling more people to attend gatherings where the gospel message is being preached or taught and that they be present as leaders minister to the needs of people.

In Mark 6, something amazing happens. Jesus' disciples followed him to his hometown where Jesus began to teach in the synagogue, and his disciples were present. Those listening to Jesus as he taught were amazed. They were puzzled as to how Jesus could possess such wisdom and power to teach and perform miraculous signs. Because the people only thought of Jesus as the son of Joseph, the local carpenter, he couldn't perform the miracles that he was capable of because the people didn't have any faith.[1] Wisdom was present. Power was present. Faith, however, wasn't present. As such, only those who had faith were able to be ministered to and to be healed by Jesus. People were too focused on Jesus being the son of a man (and the limitations that came with him being human) rather than being focused on Jesus being the Son of God (and the power and wisdom that came with him being divine).

With Jesus' disciples having witnessed the town only able to see him as the son of man, Jesus called the disciples together, gave them the same power he possessed as the Son of God, and then sent *them* out to share the message of the gospel and to perform the miraculous signs that they had been watching

---

1. Mark 6:5

him do.¹ The results are evident as they were now empowered to share the message of the gospel, cast out demons, and heal sick people.²

It was now time for the disciples to make their own decision regarding whom Jesus was. Jesus had called these young men to follow him, and he told them he would make them to become sons of men who could have the same authority as the Son of God. The disciples had only been following Jesus a brief time. They had seen and heard Jesus' "show-and-tell" presentation method. Jesus now wanted his disciples to know that, if they had faith, he had the authority to give them the same ability to say and do what he had been doing. When disciples have complete faith in Jesus, they are also given the opportunity to have the same power to perform the miraculous as Jesus did.

By sending out the twelve, Jesus would be drawing a distinction between those who thought they were disciples because they followed (*opiso*) him and those who really were his disciples because they followed (*akoloutheo*) him and imitated him. You can't imitate what you haven't seen and what you don't have faith in. So, it's important to follow Jesus and attend gatherings where his teachings are presented. We must read the Bible and pray to understand what we're called as disciples to imitate.

But for the church leader who wants to make disciples according to Jesus' standards, we must do more than encourage people to faithfully attend church services, events, and programs. We must do more than teach people to strengthen their internal spirit-man as Jesus did, as well as their external participation in the mission of God through their own ministry passions, giftings, and human strengths. Yes, yes, and yes, to all the above as a part of disciple-making which (to varying

---

1. Mark 6:7,11

2. Mark 6:12-13

Construction Phase #2: FRAMING

degrees) churches are doing to fulfill the Great Commission! But there is still more.

The Swimmer's Body Illusion is at work in discipleship if we think that disciples will be made when we do *only* these things. We can't look like Jesus and be "the body of Christ" if we're not also operating in the power that only he can give us to do the things he said his disciples, endued with power, would be able to do. These include performing miraculous signs such as casting out demons, speaking in new languages,[1] healing the sick, and raising the dead.[2] We can only operate in this kind of power if we have the kind of faith that matches it.

Jesus said to his disciples:

> I tell you for certain that <u>if you have faith in me, you will do the same things that I am doing</u>. You will even do greater things, now that I am going back to the Father. Ask me, and I will do whatever you ask. This way the Son will bring honor to the Father. I will do whatever you ask me to do.
>
> Jesus said to his disciples: "If you love me, you will do as I command. Then I will ask the Father to send you the Holy Spirit who will help you and always be with you. The Spirit will show you what is true. The people of this world cannot accept the Spirit, because they don't see

---

1. Jesus said that disciples would speak in new languages <u>before</u> the outpouring of the Holy Spirit on the day of Pentecost in Acts chapter 2. If he gave the command in Matthew 28:19-20 to "Go and make disciples," and in Mark 16:17-18 said that the sign of speaking in new languages would be one of many signs that would accompany those who are believers in him, the supernatural sign of speaking in new languages is still a sign that should function as an indicator of someone who is a Spirit-empowered disciple of Jesus today.

2. Mark 16:17, Matthew 10:6

> or know him. But you know the Spirit, who is with you and will keep on living in you...
> But the Holy Spirit will come and help you, because the Father will send the Spirit to take my place. The Spirit will teach you everything and will remind you of what I said while I was with you."[1]

Faith is necessary for God's power to be displayed. While faith is required for those who need a miracle to be able to receive it, faith is also required when it comes to disciples acting in power to do the miraculous. Faith is required to both receive and perform miracles. While this passage says that faith will enable us to do the same things Jesus did, Jesus also told us that the power of the Holy Spirit is what makes the miraculous possible.

The Holy Spirit was promised to us by Jesus so that he would continually be with us. He would continue to empower disciples to do even more miraculous things than Jesus did (I cannot imagine what could be a more miraculous display of power than raising the dead!). I'm afraid that, unless disciples return to having faith in and operating in the power of God, we may forget that he gave us access to the same power he had through the Holy Spirit, and we may continue to view the miraculous as something that only Jesus can do.

When today's disciple-making strategy is compared to how Jesus made his disciples, there is something missing. How soon after someone has come to Christ do we send them out to go and tell others the Good News and to heal the sick and cast out demons? It seems that the only expectation today's church leaders/disciple makers have for new disciples is for them to faithfully attend services, programs, and events, and to begin to cultivate spiritual strength in the interior/exterior dimensions

---

1. John 14:12-17, 26 (CEV)

of their spiritual life. Disciple makers don't have much of an expectation for new disciples to seek out opportunities to enact their faith as they go throughout their day and use the power available to them to communicate the Good News and perform miracles to show that they are disciples of Jesus.

Rather than the church being a *centrifugal* force (sending disciples out to display the power of God and make more disciples), churches have become a *centripetal* force, (gathering people who are disciple building into small groups and/or into classrooms to study the power they are told is available to them and to discuss what the scriptures teach about that power). But this approach doesn't have disciples coming to these gatherings with reports of how God used them during the week to heal the sick or cast out demons, nor do disciple makers expect that to happen. This is known as the *Pygmalion Effect*—when people perform in ways that are consistent of what is expected of them. There is no emphasis on training for power on the part of the disciple maker charged with making disciples. As the disciples that we're making begin to make disciples themselves, the present potential for power becomes but mere historical actuality.

Jesus reminded his disciples again of what he had previously told them[1] when he said that "The Holy Spirit will come upon you and give you power."[2] The Greek word for "power" in this verse is *dunamis* which, when inspected, means "power for performing miracles."

Jesus wasn't commissioning his disciples to go and make disciples who would merely attend public gatherings and participate in corporate worship services, events, and programs (disciple building for aesthetics). Neither was he commissioning his disciples to go and make disciples who would strengthen their own inward spiritual lives by growing in their

---

1. Mark 16:17-18
2. Acts 1:8 (CEV)

knowledge of Christ and relationship with him, and strengthen their own outward spiritual lives by serving out of their own natural strengths (disciple building for strength). He was commissioning his disciples to go and make disciples who would have the faith to operate in the power of the Holy Spirit to perform miraculous signs and wonders that would leave a wake of the supernatural following behind them, awakening unbelievers to the power of God (disciple building for power).

Training for power in discipleship has a disciple growing in their faith internally and externally while allowing the power of God to work through them. Power training necessitates training for strength in discipleship. As a result, the corporate body of Christ will quickly grow in size because of this type of training. But what type of growth will occur?

CONSTRUCTION PHASE #3:
EXTERIOR

TYPES OF GROWTH

Linear Growth

When we attempt to make disciples and help them to grow in their faith through attendance to church services, programs, and events while expecting the result to be an increase of the individual's spiritual growth and the collective numerical growth of the body of Christ, it is called *linear growth*. Linear growth can be plotted on a chart with a straight line that gradually ascends upward. It is growth that's experienced slowly over a much longer period, and it limits the strength and the power that's possible, promised and provided for to individuals and organizations.

Construction Phase #3: EXTERIOR

Tor Bair, the Head of Growth/Marketing at Enigma MPC says anything that's experiencing linear growth is dying or has been dead for years. This may describe the current state of an alarming number of disciples and the churches they attend. Just because something is growing and has gotten bigger over time doesn't mean it's healthy. In the article, "The Curse of Bigness," Christopher Ketcham cites that (at the time the article was written) thirty-four percent of Americans are overweight—and that number is growing. They're headed for an early death because of the health issues that accompany obesity.

Ketcham tells of a project that the U.S. Department of Agriculture embarked on where they genetically altered a pig embryo with a human growth gene. They were trying to produce a fast-growing super pig capable of producing more meat for consumption, thus making the raising of livestock more efficient. Pig #6707—the result of this attempt—was indeed an exceptionally large pig. However, it was incapable of reproduction, was mostly blind, and didn't have the strength to stand on its own.

If church leaders try to take the efficiency approach to disciple making and alter the disciple-making process that Christ designed and commanded,[1] we can end up making Disciple #6707. This kind of disciple will gather at the troughs of the tabernacle to grow in size and number but will be incapable of reproducing disciples, will be blind to the world's inability to see the power of Christ in them, and will end up not having the strength to stand on their own throughout their lives without the ministers and ministries of the church making it possible for them to take a stand.

---

1. "Go out and make disciples...Then disciple them. *Form them in the practices and postures that I have taught you*, and show them how to follow the commands I have laid down for you" Matthew 28:19-20 (VOICE) [emphasis added].

Soliloquy № 7

Exponential Growth

Linear discipleship growth can't keep pace with the rate of need that the world has for Christ. That's why leaders must have a disciple-making approach that is based on *exponential growth*. Rather than make disciples by herding them together under the roof of our churches and slowly growing the Kingdom by feeding people once a week from the "troughs of Truth" (linear growth by addition), we need a disciple-making approach that has disciples engaging in discipleship more than just once or twice a week at our corporate church services and small group meetings. We need a disciple-making approach that includes challenging disciples to seek out opportunities to exercise their natural/spiritual gifts and strengths through their own personal ministry outside of the church walls (exponential growth by multiplication).

To expand the base number of ministers exponentially, each disciple must be trained to continue to grow spiritually internally on their own apart from our services, events, and programs. This will produce disciples who are growing in strength (not just aesthetically) by exercising their faith. These disciples will be able to minister to others *themselves*—apart from the church—as they discover, develop, and deploy their spiritual gifts, natural gifts, personality, and passion and take part in the mission of God through their own personal ministry.

This type of discipleship process produces *healthy* disciples and results in numerical church growth that is exponential in nature. Exponential growth can only be achieved through the multiplication of disciples *by* disciples and will never be a result of ministries trying to add disciples to the church through services, events, and programs. If the church is going to make disciples the way Jesus made disciples, we can't simply have people gather to listen to the teachings of Christ and take part in the programs and ministries that the church has organized, scheduled, and promoted. Nor can we just collectively meet

Construction Phase #3: EXTERIOR

together on the weekend and feast on God's Word as presented by a wordsmith. While this is important, necessary, and commanded for disciples to do, it's not a balanced diet. Disciples must also learn to feed themselves spiritually during the week by chewing on his Word directly from the Bible and listening to his voice as he speaks directly to them in private prayer times. Disciples must do this in conjunction with exercising their faith through opportunities that aren't scheduled and organized by the church but are scheduled and organized by the Holy Spirit.

Jesus did perform miracles inside the synagogue, but most of his ministry to people was done *outside* the synagogue as opportunities to impact people's lives were more abundant. These opportunities would never have presented themselves in the synagogue. This is the main difference between linear growth and exponential growth.

Combinatorial Explosion

What could be better than exponential growth? It couldn't get any better, right?

What if I told you it *could* get better than growth achieved exponentially? Would you be willing to fulfill the Great Commission in a way that would not only get the attention of the church world but also the attention of the mainstream media, the government, and international leaders? Chris, you must be dreaming if you can imagine that one day you could view ongoing coverage of what's happening in the church every time you turned on the television to watch the news or looked at the front page of the newspaper! Perhaps a new category would be added to the local news hour—News, Sports, Church, and Weather. Can I remind you that when the Church was birthed, this was actually happening?

What had caused the Church to get the attention of the surrounding culture was that they had received the power Jesus

Soliloquy № 7

had promised to give them so that they could go and do what he himself was doing—preaching the good news, healing the sick, and casting out demons. The disciples had breached the banks of exponential growth and were now operating in another type of growth called *combinatorial explosion*.

A combinatorial explosion refers to a situation where an increase in the number of contributing components increases the number of possible configurations of those components and causes incredibly rapid growth. When just a few key contributing factors are combined in different configurations, not only does the rate of growth far exceed that of exponential growth, but so does the speed at which that growth is reached. Tor Bair says, "The reason for the huge disparity between growth rates [exponential vs. combinatorial] is clear—instead of the base unit increasing exponentially, the number of possible paths or connections between base units is increasing exponentially."

When Lou Hamou-Lhadj and Jacob Speirs, Character Technical Directors for Disney Pixar, were working on the movie, *Wall-E*, they had to create a huge crowd of robots for scenes on board the main spacecraft, the Axiom. The robots were to be performing every task needed on the cruise ship. In thinking about the robotic equivalent of each of those jobs, it became clear to them that they would have to design more robots than could ever be created in one lifetime for this movie. Each robot performing these functions was going to need to look different. They had no idea how to design each robot individually and specifically to accomplish this task. The job was too big. But an animator by the name of Angus MacLane offered a solution to their problem using Legos.

What Angus did as a solution to their problem was to use *combinatorics*, the branch of mathematics dealing with counting and combinations. By taking ten different heads, ten different sets of arms, and ten different bodies from Lego action figures—using only these thirty pieces—he was able to create one thousand different combinations of characters. This simple solution, using combinatoric mathematics, was just what Lou and Jacob needed to create the army of robots for the movie.

A combinatorial explosion is the kind of growth that took place in the first-century church after the disciples received the power they were promised by Jesus and they acted in faith upon it. It's the type of growth that we in the modern church are not accustomed to seeing or hearing about on a regular basis. This is because the church today has all but ceased to produce disciples who have the kind of faith to believe in a miraculous and unseen power that causes this type of explosive growth to happen.

When disciples combine three contributing components together in their lives, a combinatorial explosion can take place: (1) They gather to worship together, to be taught the Word of God, and to minister to one another, (2) They personally strengthen their own spirit-man during the week in personal devotion and spiritual growth while also building relationships with people outside the church by looking for opportunities to minister to them, and (3) They are filled with the power of the Holy Spirit, acting in faith along with that power for miraculous signs and wonders to accompany their personal ministry.

On their own, each of these components can produce only so much growth in both a disciple and in a church. But when combined, neither the disciple nor the church can comprehend the growth possibilities. Factor this exponentially and you have God's discipleship plan for the church.

THE PROMISE OF POWER

Five hundred people were gathered together with Jesus at the time of his ascension. He told them to wait in Jerusalem to receive power from the Holy Spirit. Only 120 of them, however, were personally committed in obedience to what Jesus had commanded and were in the upper room when the power from the Holy Spirit was given. All 120 of them demonstrated that power by faith, and the Church grew by three thousand that day.

Remember, Jesus told the disciples that one of the signs that would accompany those who were his disciples (and believed by faith in his power) would be that they would speak in new languages.[1] We see this being fulfilled in Acts 2:4 as it says, "The Spirit took control of everyone, and they began speaking whatever languages the Spirit led them to speak" (CEV). As a result, Peter spoke with boldness to a crowd outside of where they had gathered. The crowd had heard the miraculous sign of these uncultured Galileans speaking languages they had no conceivable way of knowing. About three thousand believed the message that Peter preached and were added to the church that very same day.[2] This kind of growth can only be described as (and obtained by) combinatorial explosion.

We could still see this type of response from today's twenty-first-century disciples if we would again take Jesus' words seriously and do things his way. But this requires us to have faith. Some say that speaking in other languages was a sign that was intended for the original disciples and not for today. But Acts 2:38-39 gives evidence that says otherwise.[3] The Great Commission was also given to the original disciples. If we use the same logic for saying that the baptism in the Holy Spirit with evidence of speaking in new languages is not for today, then the Great Commission (and many other commands and promises that Jesus spoke) would also not be for today.

---

1. Mark 16:17

2. Acts 2:41

3. "And Peter said to them, 'Repent and be baptized every one of you in the name of Jesus Christ for the forgiveness of your sins, and you will receive the gift of the Holy Spirit. For the promise is for you and for your children and for all who are far off, everyone whom the Lord our God calls to himself.'"

Construction Phase #3: EXTERIOR

The kind of growth we're experiencing in the church today is largely linear growth—exponential growth at best. And we appear to be okay with that because it's the kind of growth that's comfortable. It is familiar. It is manageable, and it's something that's within *our* power to do. The church doesn't risk scaring off unbelievers with demonstrations of miraculous signs and wonders of the Holy Spirit's power because the church today has largely been scared off from putting our faith in the miraculous power of the Holy Spirit. It seems disciples and potential disciple makers are in a place of fear just like the disciples were before the Holy Spirit was given.

The Upstairs Room, Act 1: FESTIVITY

Jesus instructed two of his disciples to go into Jerusalem and prepare the Passover meal in an upstairs room owned by a man that would be carrying a jar of water.[1] This was to be a celebration gathering for Jesus and his disciples that he commissioned but that the two disciples organized. When the other ten disciples and Jesus arrived for the celebration, Jesus blessed what had been prepared. In the midst of this celebration, John's Gospel account tells us that Satan put into Judas Iscariot's heart to betray Jesus.[2]

In a similar way today, Jesus has commissioned the establishment of the Church; church leaders prepare Sunday celebration services for other disciples (along with Jesus, who blesses the preparations), and yet disciples are being lost because Satan is at work to keep them from fully following Jesus. There's more to being a disciple than merely attending services, events, and programs that celebrate the covenant Christ has made with us.

---

1. Mark 14:12-16
2. John 13:2

Soliloquy № 7

John's Gospel further describes the fear and uncertainty that filled the minds of the disciples regarding where Jesus was going, and they were wanting some reassurances.[1] They appear to be fearful that Jesus was going to be leaving and would never be with them again. Jesus assured them he would ask the Father to send them the Holy Spirit to be with them and to help them.[2]

It was during this festivity in the upstairs room that Jesus told his disciples there was more for them to experience as they continued to follow him. Although he would not be present with them physically, he would remain with them—literally—in Spirit. He promised he would send the Holy Spirit to comfort them and empower them.

The Upstairs Room, Act 2: FEAR

After the crucifixion and resurrection of Jesus, the disciples were hiding in the same upstairs room where they celebrated the Passover meal. Rather than being in the room for a celebration, they're now there in fear. "The disciples were afraid of the Jewish leaders, and on the evening of the same Sunday they locked themselves in a room."[3]

I'm sure they recalled the conversation Jesus had with them only three days previously as they left the upstairs room to go to the Garden of Gethsemane. Jesus was preparing his disciples for what they would soon face. He told them that those who were of this world and not of his Kingdom would hate them, that they would be mistreated just as he had been mistreated, and would do to them exactly what they had done to him.[4] They

---

1. John 14
2. John 14:15
3. John 20:19
4. John 15:19-21

would be chased out of synagogues, and those that murdered them would think they were doing God a favor.[1] Jesus could only be referencing the Jewish leaders when he spoke directly of these events.

After seeing how Jesus was killed only three days before, and with his words still echoing in their minds, we find the disciples locked in that upstairs room—afraid. Suddenly, Jesus appeared before them, even though the room was locked. Their fear turned to faith once again as he showed them his hands and side. Then something that often is overlooked by students of scripture happened. "After Jesus had greeted them again, he said, 'I am sending you, just as the Father has sent me.' Then he breathed on them and said, 'Receive the Holy Spirit.'"[2]

In the upstairs room at the Passover celebration, Jesus spoke about the Holy Spirit and the power that would be given to his disciples. Remember, in Mark 16:17, Jesus revealed to them a sign that would accompany those who have faith and operate in his power. He said he would send the Holy Spirit to comfort them and would help them to overcome their fears so they could do the miraculous as he would be commissioning them to do.

Now, in the upstairs room again for a second time, Jesus encouraged his disciples with his presence, but reminded them that they had been following him so that he could send them out. Jesus then foreshadowed an event that would take place in that same room fifty days later as he breathed on them and said, "Receive the Holy Spirit." In this second appearance by Jesus in an upstairs gathering of disciples, we find Jesus strengthening the disciples in their faith.

Many disciples are in a similar place today—behind closed doors, gathered to strengthen one another, but afraid of being sent out to operate with faith and in the power that has been

---

1. John 16
2. John 20:21

made available to us through the Holy Spirit. Like the original disciples, we may take comfort in the fact that the meeting room is familiar to us, and there are many wonderful memories that fill our minds as we think about what Jesus has said and done in our lives. We as church leaders preach about what Jesus said while he was among us. We all worship him for who he is and what he has done, is doing, and can do, but we are behind closed doors, nonetheless.

Today's Church—like the original disciples—needs Jesus to show up and breathe on us, encouraging us with the command to receive the Holy Spirit. We need the faith to be sent out and to operate in the power of the Holy Spirit. Jesus gave this gift so that the Church could experience a desperately-needed combinatorial explosion of God's power and presence in the lives of broken people in need of him—and there are broken people all around us.

The Upstairs Room, Act 3: FAITH

When Jesus first appeared to his disciples behind closed doors and breathed on them, Thomas was not present. His faith was still in a weakened state. One week later, Jesus miraculously appeared again in the all-familiar upstairs room, with the doors locked. This time Thomas was there, but he didn't yet believe that Jesus had appeared to the other disciples, or that he was actually alive. He hadn't felt the warmth of Jesus' breath as he had breathed on the other ten disciples and said that he was preparing them to receive the Holy Spirit who would comfort them and empower them.

When Jesus had appeared in their midst this time, he said to Thomas, "Stop doubting and have faith!"[1] Thomas now had the proof he said he needed before he could believe Jesus was alive,

---

1. John 20:27 (CEV)

and he professed his faith. But Jesus questioned the *source* of Thomas' faith. He asked him, "Thomas, do you have faith because you have seen me? The people who have faith in me without seeing me are the ones who are really blessed!"[1]

Again, this is where we find many disciples in the church today—behind the doors of the church, doubting the power of God to do miracles as he did, and wanting/needing proof. Normally, this is the place in which we would find people who are lost and without a relationship with God. *They* are the ones who are locked behind closed doors in their hearts, who doubt the power of God to do the miraculous, and need proof that he's alive and cares for them. But rather than this being the condition that we find the world in, it seems to be the Church that is in this condition. If the people of this world are in this place, and we who know that the power of God can do "far more abundantly than all we could ask or think, according to the power at work within us"[2] are also behind our closed doors, who do you suppose God has called to take the first step of faith to venture out from behind them?

The Upstairs Room, Act 4: FIRE

We see the first step being taken by the disciples as they once again met in that upstairs room.[3] This time they had gathered— not out of fear, but out of faith—to pray and to select a disciple who would "help us tell others that Jesus has been raised from death."[4] As they not only met together but also strengthened their internal spirit-man by praying as Jesus had demonstrated

---

1. John 20:29 (CEV)
2. Ephesians 3:20
3. Acts 1:12-24
4. Acts 1:21 (CEV)

and taught them to do, they simultaneously used the strengths of their outer natural-man to perform some church business.

Peter, using his gift of leadership, spent time studying the scripture, then led a brief "Bible study" based on what he'd been reading. Then he proceeded to conduct a business meeting that would result in raising up a disciple who would join the eleven. Shortly after Peter led this meeting, the gentle breath that Jesus had breathed on them fifty days before had swollen into a rushing, mighty windstorm that filled the upstairs room. Jesus kept his promise, and the disciples who had been filled with faith were now all filled with power. The accompanying sign of speaking with other languages (which Jesus spoke of in Mark 16:17) came upon these disciples who were embracing what would empower the combinatorial explosion of the church.

They had grown in **size** as the twelve disciples in an upstairs room increased exponentially from ten to 120 people. They were growing in **strength** as they had been praying and studying scripture on their own and using their gifts. Now, they were about to begin growing in **power** as the Holy Spirit had been sent to them as promised, and their faith in his power enabled them to operate in the supernatural with signs following. The result was not linear growth. Nor was the result exponential growth. The result was a combinatorial explosion.

Linear discipleship growth alone is never going to completely fulfill the Great Commission. It produces followers who want to be fed God's Word but never digest it or feed it to others. These followers may attend the celebration feasts and grow in faithfulness to church attendance, but they never faithfully attend to the mission of personally making disciples. For this type of believer, disciple making means inviting people who don't normally go to church to attend a service or an event with them. Since there's no personal strength training, they're too weak to stand against the tactics of the enemy. Satan can easily entice some to pursue their own selfish will rather than God's will of selflessness.

Construction Phase #3: EXTERIOR

Exponential discipleship growth is much better. While this approach to disciple building has disciples growing in spiritual strength internally through the practice of incorporating spiritual disciplines into their lives, it also has them strengthening their own abilities and talents and using them to aid in making other disciples who attend services, programs, and events. However, when these disciples encounter situations that call for the miraculous to minister through them in a situation, they're often ineffective in supernaturally breaking through strongholds that the enemy has placed in unbelievers' lives when they are outside of the church environment.

The enemy knows what would happen if we ever experienced combinatorial explosion in our discipleship growth. Satan will do anything he can to bring confusion to the doctrine of the Holy Spirit and have disciples view the Holy Spirit as irrational, unnecessary, archaic, and even demonic. But what could happen if we would just simply surrender to the power made available to all disciples, and if we would only have faith to begin to do the things Jesus said we could do under the power of the Holy Spirit?

Satan doesn't pay a whole lot of attention to slow, linear discipleship growth. That's nothing he's too uncomfortable with. It's a nuisance, and he must do a little more work to convince others to "grow comfortable in growing in comfort." He may get a little more involved when the church begins to expand the base of disciples who are engaging in spiritual disciplines and are taking part in the mission of God through a personal ministry and growing exponentially. But things that grow exponentially can un-grow exponentially. People can become unsatisfied, begin to disengage, or not engage at all with spiritual growth and serving in ministry. They can also fall away from their faith altogether. Like strong empires, such as the Roman Empire and the British Empire, strong disciples can fail in their own strength.

But when disciples begin to work from within the supernatural power of the Holy Spirit, Satan can only sit back and watch because there's nothing he can do when the Spirit of God is doing the work. Satan is afraid that disciples will discover and use that power. It seems he has *convinced* a large number of disciples to be afraid to discover and operate in the power of the Holy Spirit as well. The devil is the one who hides behind locked doors when we come out from behind them with the faith to operate in the power of the Holy Spirit.

CONSTRUCTION PHASE #4:
INTERIOR

THE CHURCH, INC.

Both the Church and the business world have a lot in common. The Church attempts to operate like an organization by maximizing the efficiency of its operations, while businesses attempt to operate like a church by making people feel more like they are a part of a family and creating customers who become vocal evangelists and dedicated disciples of their brands and products. As such, the Church has been approaching growth in much the same way that businesses do. Andrew Miller, the Head of Growth for *Enter, Inc.*, began an article he wrote for *Forbes Magazine* with a thought that seems to parallel the model of discipleship that Jesus began. He writes,

> In the early stages of a business, the drivers of growth are usually inherited in the founder's philosophy, mission and practices. At this stage, your goals are clear, your team is small.

Construction Phase #4: INTERIOR

Jesus never intended for us to stray away from this growth model. When it comes to disciple-making, scripture is clear as to what Jesus' philosophy, mission, and practices were and still are today:
- *Philosophy*: Have faith in the power of God.
- *Mission*: Go make disciples.
- *Practices*: Preach the gospel and perform signs and wonders.

Miller goes on to describe five central business growth strategies that we can see church leaders adopting as growth models today. In fact, it is possible to see Jesus using the first three in his own ministry.

#1: Market Penetration

The first growth strategy is "Market Penetration." Miller writes that, in this strategy, a product or service gets introduced into a market where there's some competition. Growth in this context happens when you differentiate yourself from those competing with you. What will give a business an edge over their competitors is that they meet people's needs better than anyone else or focus on a "specific underserved niche" as Miller calls it.

Do you see the similarities in this strategy with what Jesus did in his ministry on earth? Church planters seem to fall into this category of growth strategy, but many churches are also constantly assessing their ministry effectiveness and making modifications to how they minister to people, which keeps them penetrating the market with the gospel in effective and meaningful ways.

Soliloquy № 7

#2: Audience Expansion

A second growth strategy is "Audience Expansion." This is a tactic where a business offers its products or services in a new location. Businesses whose brand has become well-known will often expand their brand to a new area by offering franchise options to others who will open new areas for the brand to be introduced into.

Jesus also did this as he began to expand his ministry to other towns in the region by commissioning people he had ministered to, such as the demon-possessed man he healed and sent back to minister to his own family.[1] This qualifies as exponential growth because the base of ministers is expanded, and ministry is taken to places where the church may never would have been given the opportunity to minister.

#3: Product Line Expansion

A third growth strategy is "Product Line Expansion." This strategy has businesses offering variations of their core product so they can market those variations to different segments of society.

While Jesus never strayed from the message that he was the Son of God who was sent to seek and save the lost, the message was presented in a variety of ways. Jesus presented the message to fishermen by giving them fishing examples, and gave farming illustrations to farmers, etc. He expounded on fulfilling the commandments, not only through the law but also through grace, all the while keeping the message central to the gospel. The church continues to do this today by ministering to specific groups of people, such as through a youth ministry's small group for teenage girls who are in junior high

---

1. Mark 5:19

Construction Phase #4: INTERIOR

school, or through a support group for recovering addicts, or to single parents.

The next two growth strategies are being attempted by the twenty-first-century church, but there is no indication that Jesus used either of these growth strategies. However, there may be nothing wrong with the church adopting them as Jesus did not say we were limited to doing only the things he did and in the same way that he did them.

#4: Product & Market Diversification

The fourth growth strategy Miller mentions is "Product and Market Diversification." Businesses will often get into selling new products or services that are unrelated to the core of their business in an attempt to expand the reach of their profits by using the stability of their core business to facilitate the diversification. One example of a business that tried to introduce a service that was unrelated to their business was Hooters Air, an airline business started by Hooters of America to promote their chain of Hooters restaurants.

It seems that, as churches and their leaders begin to rely less on faith and operating in the power of the supernatural, they look for ways to impact the community around them with methods that will get the attention of the world. These are done in the name of the gospel and are embarked upon in faith, but they don't leave the world standing in amazement and asking, "Who is this Jesus?" If such methods worked better than Spirit-empowered signs and wonders, Jesus could have changed the world through his carpentry business by building houses for the homeless.

Churches may enter into diversified ministries with good intentions, such as operating orphanages, hospitals, and day-cares, and building and running housing developments for low-income individuals. These are a ministry of the church intended to serve the needs of people. I'm *not* saying that the church shouldn't diversify into these kinds of endeavors to reach people at their point of need. But, if we abandon the unashamed communication of the Good News and cease to have the faith for signs and wonders to accompany us as believers in favor of these kinds of diversified ministries, the Church may find itself becoming more focused on ministry diversification rather than on the centralization of our mission: making disciples who are growing in power, strength, and size.

Truthfully, we need both. We seem to have a tough time balancing our attention between the natural (which we seemingly can control) and the supernatural (which we definitely can't control).

#5: Acquisition & Merger

The final growth strategy Miller writes about is "Acquisition and Merger." Businesses will often buy other businesses that produce products that have made a name for themselves. It would cost the parent company a fortune in research and development to make the same product that was as good as or better than the company to be acquired is making. This can be illustrated in the case of Apple Computer buying Beats Electronics who were making headphones that were far superior to the ones Apple had been shipping with their products.

Will the day come when churches start to make this a primary strategy of numerical growth — acquiring other parachurch ministries who are being missionally-effective, or even other churches who own campuses in prime, high-cost locations but are in financial distress? We have already seen the phenomena of multi-site "franchised" churches causing miraculous numerical church growth in areas where already-established churches have had little to no success in church growth or in making disciples. If we aren't careful, we may inadvertently become subscribers to a type of architectural determinism that would cause us to base our disciple-making efforts on franchising, acquiring, or merging ministries like businesses do. Rather than creating disciples who will personally go and find those who haven't heard the gospel message and penetrating people's hearts with the gospel through the power of the Holy Spirit, we may find it easier to acquire or create ministries than to do what disciples were intended to do.

Let's not fall for the Swimmer's Body Illusion that would lead us to believe that if we can just get people into the "pool" of a church that their participation in the life of the church will result in producing a church body of disciples that resembles the body of Christ. Spirit-empowered disciples resemble the body of Christ and is what we are called to make. The world may never come to our church buildings to be ministered to. We must remain focused on expanding our ministry in ways that are far beyond our capabilities as humans and are only possible through spirit-empowered disciples.

If we want to experience combinatorial growth in disciple making, we must employ more than business tactics for our churches and the people of our churches to grow. In order to see supernatural growth in both disciples and our churches, we *must* grow in our faith and in the power of the supernatural. Growing in strength alone will not produce combinatorial explosive growth.

LESSON FROM ZECHARIAH

To give a picture of this, and from an Old Testament perspective, let's look to Zechariah 4:1-7:

> And the angel who talked with me came again and woke me, like a man who is awakened out of his sleep. And he said to me, "What do you see?"

Soliloquy № 7

> I said, "I see, and behold, a lampstand of all gold, with a bowl on top of it, and seven lamps on it, with seven lips on each of the lamps that are on top of it. And there are two olive trees by it, one on the right of the bowl and the other on its left." And I said to the angel who talked with me, "What are these, my lord?" Then the angel who talked with me answered and said to me, "Do you not know what these are?" I said, "No, my lord." Then he said to me, "This is the word of the LORD to Zerubbabel: Not by might, nor by power, but by my Spirit, says the LORD of hosts. Who are you, O great mountain? Before Zerubbabel you shall become a plain."

As Zechariah was awakened by an angel, he saw a lampstand which was a familiar item of furniture from the temple. What wasn't familiar to him were the two olive trees, one on either side of the lampstand. They were each continually supplying oil to the bowl of the lampstand through two golden pipes—one pipe from each olive tree—and the oil provided the seven lips of the lamps that were on it with a constant supply of oil for their light to remain illuminated.

In the tabernacle, one of the jobs of the priests was to ensure that the lamps were continually supplied with oil. But what Zechariah saw was this lampstand was constantly being supplied with oil from the two olive trees. In Zechariah 4:11-14, the prophet inquired of the angel what the two olive trees represented. The angel replied that they were "the two anointed ones who stand by the Lord of the whole earth."

Ellen White writes this of the explanation of the two olive trees in her book, *The Great Controversy*:

> Concerning the two witnesses, the prophet declares further: "These are the two olive trees,

Construction Phase #4: INTERIOR

and the two candlesticks standing before the God of the earth." "Thy Word," says the psalmist, "is a lamp unto my feet, and a light unto my path." (Revelation 11:4; Psalms 119:105). The two witnesses represent the Scriptures of the Old and the New Testament. Both are important testimonies to the origin and perpetuality of the law of God. Both are witnesses also to the plan of salvation. The types, sacrifices, and prophecies of the Old Testament point forward to a Saviour to come. The Gospel and Epistles of the New Testament tell of a Saviour who has come in the exact manner foretold by type and prophecy.

It's the Holy Spirit of God that gives us the power to overthrow mountains. Like the oil lamp, the Holy Spirit is the oil that flows through the wick so the wick doesn't burn in its own strength and power, but it's the oil that's moving *through* the wick and is set aflame. A picture of this is given in Acts 2 when the Holy Spirit filled the disciples and on top of their heads appeared burning tongues of fire. They spoke in other languages as they allowed the Holy Spirit to flow *through* them. From the Word of God flows the Spirit of God. When the "lips" of human lamps allow the Holy Spirit to flow through them, as evidenced by initially speaking in other languages and then continually through signs and wonders done through the power of the Holy Spirit, the power of God can fill the church and move mountains.

The Church/Lampstand

In Revelation 1:12-20, John saw seven golden lampstands with Jesus in the middle of them. His right hand held seven stars. Jesus explained to John that the seven stars were the

Soliloquy № 7

seven angels, or "messengers"—pastors of the churches, and the seven lampstands were the seven churches. The lips of the leaders of our churches have the responsibility to preach the whole gospel and not hold back the work of the Holy Spirit.[1]

If we lead our churches and ministries and attempt to make disciples but leave out the Holy Spirit that Jesus sent to us in his fullness, what will the consequences be when we stand before God in taking responsibility for those disciples that we made but withheld from them knowledge of and encouragement to be filled with the power of the Holy Spirit? The world doesn't need large, aesthetically pleasing churches that are full of people who are growing in relationship and service to both God and man in their own strength. What the world needs are churches of *any* size filled with willing disciples who have *any* level of personal ability but are full of faith in God's power to bring the light of the gospel to a dark world. In her book, *Testimonies to Ministers and Gospel Workers,* Ellen White writes:

> The Holy Spirit is doing its [His] work on the hearts. But if the ministers have not first received their message from heaven, if they have not drawn their own supplies from the refreshing, life-giving stream, how can they let that flow forth which they have not received? What a thought, that hungry, thirsty souls are sent away empty! A man may lavish all the treasures of his learning, he may exhaust the moral engines of his nature, and yet accomplish nothing, because he himself has not received the golden oil from the heavenly messengers; therefore, it cannot flow forth from him, imparting spiritual life to the needy. The tidings of joy and hope must

---

1. 1 Thessalonians 5:19

come from heaven. Learn, oh, learn of Jesus
what it means to abide in Christ!

It was during the time of Zechariah's vision that the Israelites had just returned to Jerusalem from exile. As they were trying to rebuild the temple, they were experiencing an enormous amount of adversity from Satan directly, and through others such as Sanballat, who opposed the rebuilding of the temple. In as much, their work had been halted due to discouragement and fear. God wanted the temple to be restored so it could resume its function as a place of worship, so God called the prophet Zechariah to deliver a message of hope and encouragement for God's people to renew their work. The visions God was giving to Zechariah conveyed that it wasn't going to be by the might of the people, nor the power that they could attain or possess, but it would only be by the work of the Holy Spirit that the rebuilding of the temple would be accomplished.

It's not hard to see the parallel between the problem that Israel was facing in rebuilding the temple and the hearts of disciples today. God is wanting his temple to be built in the lives of his disciples, and there's a lot of adversity from Satan and the "kingdoms of this world" to prevent that from happening. Discouragement and fear can grip disciples who would take on the challenge of becoming the temple of the Holy Spirit.[1] It will not be by our might or our power, but by the power of the Holy Spirit that his temple will be built for us to resume the function that he commanded us as disciples to do.

The work to become the type of disciple who would function as Christ laid out in the Gospels seems so massive and impossible under our own attempts. The task seems like a great mountain that needs to be moved. It's only when the power of the Holy Spirit is at work in us that the mountain can be moved. Ellen White says in her book *True Revival*:

---

1. 1 Corinthians 6:19

Soliloquy № 7

There is nothing that Satan fears so much as that the people of God shall clear the way by removing every hindrance, so that the Lord can pour out His Spirit upon a languishing church and an impenitent congregation. If Satan had his way, there would never be another awakening, great or small, to the end of time. But we are not ignorant of his devices. It is possible to resist his power. When the way is prepared for the Spirit of God, the blessing will come. Satan can no more hinder a shower of blessing from descending upon God's people than he can close the windows of heaven that rain cannot come upon the earth. Wicked men and devils cannot hinder the work of God, or shut out His presence from the assemblies of His people, if they will, with subdued, contrite hearts, confess and put away their sins, and in faith claim His promises. Every temptation, every opposing influence, whether open or secret, may be successfully resisted, "Not by might, nor by power, but by my Spirit, saith the Lord of Hosts" (Zechariah 4:6).

Disciples have the capability to become mountain-movers when they operate with the power provided to them through the Holy Spirit. When they're spiritually transformed through the process of genuine, authentic, and biblical discipleship, they have the capability of developing the "swimmer's body" of Christ and look like him, develop their strength in spiritual and natural ways, and operate in the power that he gives to them through the Holy Spirit. This is how we will see supernatural, combinatorial explosive growth—not only in disciples' lives, but also in our churches as well.

GOD THE ARCHITECT

In his book, *Architects on Architecture*, Paul Heyer provides a quote from Minoru Yamasaki, the architect of Pruitt-Igoe who believed in architectural determinism and that building design could change people. Incidentally, Yamasaki was also the architect of the famous Twin Towers in New York City that were the target of terrorist attacks on September 11, 2001. Yamasaki said this at the opening of the World Trade Center on April 4, 1973:

> There are a few very influential architects who sincerely believe that all buildings must be "strong." The word "strong" in this context seems to connote "powerful"—that is, each building should be a monument to the virility of our society. These architects look with derision upon attempts to build a friendly, more gentle kind of building. The basis for their belief is that our culture is derived primarily from Europe, and that most of the important traditional examples of European architecture are monumental, reflecting the need of the state, church, or the feudal families—the primary patrons of these buildings—to awe and impress the masses. This is incongruous today. Although it is inevitable for architects who admire these great monumental buildings of Europe to strive for the quality most evident in them—grandeur, the elements of mysticism and power, basic to cathedrals and palaces, are also incongruous today, because the buildings we build for our times are for a totally different purpose.

If we were to impose what Yamasaki said here about physical buildings onto disciples who are the temple of the Holy

Spirit, the message would be that we don't need disciples who are strong or powerful, but who are merely friendly and gentle in "e-lite" ways (see chapter 2). It would mean that the power of God is no longer needed to awe and impress the masses. Striving to make disciples who are filled with the qualities that embody the grandeur and power of God is no longer necessary because that kind of disciple is no longer needed. It would mean that the disciples that the Church builds today are for a totally different purpose. People would be idealistically transformed through a disciple-making design that was friendly and gentle, powerless, and weak.

While disciples must be friendly and gentle with people in the natural realm, they must also be strong and powerful in the supernatural realm. If the masses of the world are ever in need of being in awe and impressed by the power of God given to his disciples through the Holy Spirit for the building of his Church, it's now. First-century disciples—like European cathedrals—need to be constructed once more with strength and power as a monument to the power that God has given to disciples to fulfill his mission. We shouldn't attempt to make disciples for a purpose other than what God intended. The purpose of disciple making is fixed, not fluid. We as church leaders must have our gaze fixed on God's plan for making disciples and not take our eyes off that plan.

Admonishment #3: Be committed to the mission of making empowered disciples the way that Jesus made them. This must include the often discounted, neglected, and overlooked aspect of Spirit-baptism with the initial physical evidence of speaking in other languages which was a critical component of God's disciple-making design for combinatorial explosion.

Construction Phase #4: INTERIOR

Questions:

- Do you subscribe to the theory of architectural determinism in a spiritual sense, promoting the belief that if people will simply attend our church services or programs being held in our buildings that people will change into disciples of Christ?
- How has the Swimmer's Body Illusion affected you in your disciple-making efforts and in your own personal discipleship?
- Are you making aesthetic disciples, strong disciples, or powerful disciples?
- How will the disciples you are making feel when they find out that they could have been more fruitful and their reward could have been so much greater if they would have been trained to operate in the power of the Spirit and not just the strength of the self?
- Is your ministry making disciples linearly or are your disciples making disciples exponentially?
- Why are most of our modern-day churches modeled after the practices of the early church in Acts 2:42-47 but ignore the power that made those practices effective in Acts 2:4?
- Is your faith in the power of God and *all* that he can do (which is far beyond what you could imagine as possible) at its fullest, and if so, are signs and wonders accompanying your ministry as commonly as you use the gifts and talents he's given you the power to do?

"Watch where you are going! Stick to the path of truth, and the road will be safe and smooth before you."

Proverbs 4:26, (TPT)

Four

DESERT SAND THROUGH THE HOURGLASS:
Staying on the Path & the Black Swan Theory

> *"The greatest obstacle to living is expectancy, which hangs upon tomorrow and loses today. You are arranging what lies in Fortune's control, and abandoning what lies in yours. What are you looking at? To what goal are you straining? The whole future lies in uncertainty: live immediately."*
>
> —Seneca, *On the Shortness of Life*

Soliloquy № 7

CAIRN MARKER #1:
A MIRAGE IN THE DESERT

THE TARTAR STEPPE

In 1935, Dino Buzzati wrote a story entitled *Il deserto dei Tartari* (translated "The Desert of the Tartars). I own an original copy of the English translation, *The Tartar Steppe*. It's a fictional story about a young lieutenant named Giovanni Drogo who had recently graduated from the Royal Military Academy. He had been assigned to his first post, the Bastiani Fortress. It was a small, second class fort that lay on the border between Giovanni's country and that of the Tartars. The fort, which guarded a mountain pass, was situated atop a sloping plateau, and was flanked by tall mountains on either side that overlooked a great desert. It was located in a place so desolate that those Drogo met along the way to ask for directions knew nothing about the fort and even denied that it existed at all. The Bastiani Fortress was all but forgotten.

It had been more than one hundred years since anyone at the fort had seen the Tartars in the region. For this to be the first assignment for a young military officer who had envisioned being engaged in battles and becoming a decorated soldier, the post was underwhelming to say the least. Needless to say, Giovanni didn't want to remain stationed there. Buzzati wrote, "If only he could turn back, not even cross the threshold of the Fort but ride back down to the plain, to his own city, to his old habits. Such was Drogo's first thought; and, however shameful such weakness in a soldier, he was ready to confess to it, if necessary, provided they let him go at once."

Giovanni entered the fort and presented his orders to the major who oversaw personnel. Drogo began to explain that he hadn't requested to be posted at the fortress, and that he was

Cairn Marker #1: A MIRAGE IN THE DESERT

determined to be transferred as soon as was possible. The major appeared to not be interested in Giovanni's disappointment. He recalled that he knew the lieutenant's father and voiced his optimism that he would live up to the memory that the major had of him. Giovanni resumed his appeal to the major for being transferred. To his surprise, the major began to search for the best solution to Giovanni's request.

The major eventually convinced Giovanni to remain at the fort for four months. Then he was to see the doctor who could process the transfer based on a contrived sickness. Before he had left the major's office, Giovanni requested to be able to look over the north wall of the fort to see the desert which he'd never seen. The major explained to him that his request could not be granted as only personnel who were on duty could enter the areas where a view of the desert was possible. As Giovanni left he discovered that the only way one could see the expanse was from the New Redoubt which was a part of the fort that lay on the peak. Only those who were assigned to that area had ever seen the desert.

After the four months had passed, Giovanni saw the doctor and was granted the certificate that would enable his transfer. But after seeing the snow-laden fort in the winter as the sun had illuminated it in all white, hearing the sounds of the trumpets in a new tone, and seeing the bayonets of the soldiers shimmering in bright silver, he determined that he couldn't leave the fort. He was captivated by the mystery of the fort's mission of remaining vigilant against an attack by the Tartars from the desert.

Two years later, Giovanni found himself in command of the New Redoubt and was in charge of keeping watch for the invading Tartars. It was the most isolated outlying part of the Bastiani Fortress complex, an hour's walk from the main fort. Since no one had seen the Tartar's from the fort for over a century, you can imagine that life at the fort was full of the mundane. Giovanni soon found himself forming the habit of daydreaming each evening. He would imagine a great battle where he and a few of his men held off thousands of Tartars. With his ammunition running low and wounded by a missile, reinforcements would arrive on the scene and the enemy would retreat. As he collapses in exhaustion, he's roused by someone calling his name. He opens his eyes to see the king himself bending over him and saying, "Well done!"

This was, of course, just a daydream.

Some thirty years passed as Giovanni spent each day the same as the last. Meanwhile, his friends back in the city had married, raised children, and lived rich, textured lives with lots of events to reflect upon during their old age. Giovanni had spent his life in one long, patient vigil, waiting for an event that hadn't happened in the past century and may not happen for another. But by the end of the book, the Tartars did appear on the horizon of the desert and attack the fort. Up to this point, no one alive had ever seen the Tartars or had known of anyone from the past who had either. The men of the fort—including Giovanni—faithfully continued to be vigilant in what they had been assigned to do which was to watch for the Tartars and be prepared to fight them.

Buzzati never wrote whether the men of Fort Bastiani were able defend their country from the attacking Tartars and win the battle. Whether they won that battle was not the point of his story. Giovanni was a hero in his own right because of how he lived his life while at the fort. As Nassim Nicholas Taleb writes in his book, *Fooled by Randomness: The Hidden Role of Chance in Life and in the Markets*, "Heroes are Heroes because they are heroic in behavior, not because they won or lost."

THE BLACK SWAN THEORY

When you think of a swan, the image comes to mind of a big, white bird with a long neck and orange-yellowish beak,

Cairn Marker #1: A MIRAGE IN THE DESERT

accented by an outline of black that apexes at the eyes. No one imagines a big, black bird with accentuated white pennaceous flight feathers, having a long neck and a red beak with a white tip that apexes at the eyes.

All swans are white, right?

Up until 1697, when a group of Dutch explorers led by Willem de Vlamingh discovered the western side of Australia, everyone in Europe believed all swans were white. Vlamingh was the first European to set foot in Australia and find out that not all swans were white. He returned to Europe with a few of the black swans he had captured.

A black swan

The poet Juvenal wrote in the second century: "Rara avis in terries nigroque simillima cygno" ("A rare bird in the lands and very much like a black swan"). Juvenal is credited as having coined the term "Black Swan" and correlating it to a rare and unlikely event, because—in the second century—black swans were presumed to be nonexistent. Up until the sixteenth century,

Soliloquy № 7

Europeans were using the phrase when they described something that was impossible. Today, this phrase has come to characterize something that's extremely rare and unlikely.

Nassim Nicholas Taleb has developed the Black Swan Theory and uses the term "Black Swans" to describe events that are rare, hard to predict, and beyond the realm of normal expectations. In his book, *The Black Swan: The Impact of the Highly Improbable*, He writes:

> What we call here a Black Swan (and capitalize it) is an event with the following three attributes.
>
> First, it is an outlier, as it lies outside the realm of regular expectations, because nothing in the past can convincingly point to its possibility. Second, it carries an extreme 'impact'. Third, in spite of its outlier status, human nature makes us connect explanations for its occurrence after the fact, making it explainable and predictable.
>
> I stop here and summarize the triplet: rarity, extreme 'impact', and retrospective (though not prospective) predictability. A small number of Black Swans explains almost everything in our world, from the success of ideas and religions, to the dynamics of historical events, to elements of our own personal lives.

So according to Taleb, the three criteria of a Black Swan event are: (1) the event has to be a shocker to everyone because it could not have been predicted by anyone (2) the event has to have a major impact on current and/or future people and/

or events, and (3) after the event has happened, the *Hindsight bias*[1] has people rationalizing the event.

Taleb gave some examples in his book of Black Swan events with these characteristics: the rise and implementation of the internet in our society, the adoption of the personal computer as a household staple, World War I, the Soviet Union being dissolved, and the attacks on the World Trade Center/Pentagon on September 11, 2001. He could have very well included an attack by the mysterious Tartars who were never reported to have been seen. Being the forerunner of the development of the Black Swan theory, Taleb cites an excellent example that really helps us to clearly understand Black Swan events:

> Consider a turkey that is fed every day. Every single feeding will firm up the bird's belief that it is the general rule of life to be fed every day by friendly members of the human race. On the afternoon of the Wednesday before Thanksgiving, something unexpected will happen to the turkey. It will incur a revision of belief.

To the turkey, Thanksgiving Day is a Black Swan event. To the butcher who's been feeding the turkey for a year, Thanksgiving Day has been a planned event all along. Black Swan events take observers (not orchestrators) by surprise.

There are so many events that occur in your life that you can never predict. You go through your life, living one day to the next with some idea of how you envision each day will play out. But, inevitably, events occur in your life that you could

---

1. *Hindsight bias* is a psychological term used to explain the phenomenon of people who, after an unpredictable event has occurred, believe that they had predicted the outcome when, in fact, there was no way for the outcome of the event to have been predicted by anyone.

Soliloquy № 7

never have planned for or predicted. You know as a believer in Christ that God is not taken by surprise, and he has orchestrated the events of your life. The psalmist David wrote, "All the days planned for me were written in your book before I was one day old."[1] With all of the wisdom and intelligence we humans *think* we've amassed which make us feel superior to anything else on earth, we can't be the orchestrators of our own lives and shield ourselves from Black Swan events. We can't predict these kinds of events, and we have no control over them.

What Does the Future Hold?

At the University of Pennsylvania, psychologist Philip Tetlock embarked on a twenty-year study to find out if people who were knowledgeable about past events could use that knowledge to predict the outcomes of future events. He published the findings in his book, *Expert Political Judgement: How Good Is It? How Can We Know?* The book offered proof that "experts" are *terrible* at predicting Black Swan events.

In his research, Tetlock interviewed 284 men and women whose profession was "commenting or offering advice on political and economic trends." They were asked to examine known events that would be taking place in a relatively short matter of time—events that would happen in parts of the world these men and women considered themselves to be knowledgeable as well as parts of the world that they had no expertise—and assess the likelihood of one of three outcomes occurring for them.

In all, Tetlock gathered more than eighty thousand predictions. When the results were tallied, the predictions of the so-called "experts" were as accurate as if they would have just evenly distributed their predictions to each of the three outcomes. Even those who had no knowledge of what was

---

1. Psalms 139:16 (NCV)

Cairn Marker #1: A MIRAGE IN THE DESERT

happening in certain parts of the world predicted the outcome almost as well as the experts did. In other words, the expert predictions were terrible! In fact, the more knowledge the expert had of an area, the less reliable the prediction, even though their predictions were just a little better than those who had no knowledge of that area whatsoever.

Nobel laureate Daniel Kahneman called this effect "The Illusion of Pundits" in his book, *Thinking, Fast and Slow*. He writes, "The illusion that we understand the past fosters overconfidence in our ability to predict the future." What is certain is that experts can't predict the future based on the past. We tend to believe that we can confidently peer into the future and predict the events of our lives based on the clarity of our knowledge of the past because "hindsight is 20/20."

It appears that even with the seemingly complete knowledge of ornithology that Europeans had amassed at the time, they had no idea until 1697 that, somewhere in the world, there were indeed, black swans. While we don't have any success at controlling the events of the future, the only thing that we can have any success at controlling is how we'll choose to live when we face unpredictable Black Swan events.

Butterflies Messed Up My Plans

It's impossible for your life to have complete predictability and go according to the plans you've made for yourself. The decision that's made by a person halfway around the world, as well as by a person in your own home, can bring surprising and tremendous changes that can alter *your* "perfect" plans. It's a concept known as the *Butterfly Effect*.

While this term originates from the idea that a butterfly flapping its wings in South America could affect the weather on another continent and is used in chaos theory, it's a way of describing how macrosystems with too many variables can be

Soliloquy № 7

unpredictable because of the many microsystems that can affect the accuracy of predictability. I was once talking with my mom about some event taking place in my life that was outside my everyday routine. She mentioned that life would soon get back to normal. I mused, "What is *normal?*" and continued by saying that everyone would have to agree to *my* idea of what normal is in order for my life to ever be normal!

Truly, there are times when it seems everything is great and going according to *your* plan. Sometimes things are just how you would have them to be. Then, just when everything is *normal* for you, some unforeseen circumstance enters your life that messes everything up (even your own feelings and perceptions). That's when frustration, discouragement and despair can enter the space between your ears.

This can be especially true in the life of a church leader. We set goals for ourselves and our ministries. Then, we create a five or ten-year strategic plan to carry out those goals. When things don't go according to the "plan," we feel as though we've somehow failed. That's when we feel like either giving up, quitting, or going somewhere else where the people and the conditions may be more favorable for our plans to be accomplished. "We can make our plans, but the LORD determines our steps."[1]

I would like to believe that all the plans I make for my life and ministry have been given to me from the Lord. Ultimately, whatever plans I make or think God has given to me, he often doesn't fully reveal them to me—for my life or for my ministry. He does direct my steps—no matter what plans I might have made or may believe that he's given me. God's plan seems to be simply for me to trust, obey, and follow him every step of the way and leave the planning up to him.

As we discussed in chapter 3, the church and church leadership function much like businesses and their management do

---

1. Proverbs 16:9 (NLT)

in many ways. There is a lot of room for businesses to "manipulate" the human brain (through marketing techniques and the use of various forms of psychology) and manufacture results through human efforts. The church and its leadership sometimes have trouble distinguishing instances when the church functions as a business—doing things that are dependent upon human efforts—and when it doesn't. The Church belongs to Christ, and he builds it. It's not up to church leaders to build *his* Church.

In both church and business, we may try to figure out a strategic plan that will get us to where we want to go, but the fact remains that we have no idea what ten years from now—five years from now—even next year—will be like. While businesspeople can create a strategic plan, pursue it, and alter things to adapt to the changes in market conditions and needs, church leaders must be sensitive to the Holy Spirit and follow his leading. He knows the future (which is uncertain to us) and wants to guide us in the present towards the future of which he is certain.

William Starbuck in his article, *Payoffs and Pitfalls of Strategic Learning,* writes that one of the downsides to strategic planning is that, as businesses move into the future, they can become saddled by a plan that was conceptualized in the past but may no longer be relevant. Rather than maintain flexibility to unforeseen changes, they keep pursuing their out-of-date "ten-year strategic plan." If other options came along that would be better for business, they often go overlooked or ignored because of the sacredness of the strategic plan.

To give a few examples from the past of businesses that *were* flexible and didn't stick to their strategic plan, in his book, *Antifragile: Things That Gain from Disorder,* Nassim Nicholas Taleb cites instances of businesses that started with a plan to produce a certain product but ended up in a completely different business. Coca-Cola began as a pharmaceutical product and ended up a soft drink company. Tiffany &

Soliloquy № 7

Co. started as a stationery store and evolved into a luxury jewelry and goods retailer. Raytheon was making refrigerators and somehow ended up manufacturing the first missile guidance system. Nokia was founded in 1865 as a paper mill and, as time passed, ended up making mobile phones. Avon began as a door-to-door book sales company, and although the door-to-door sales method was kept, they transitioned to selling beauty, cosmetics, and household items.

If you as a church leader rely more on business practices and less on following God's plan each day, you will later discover that the strategic plan you have for your life or ministry had been erroneously designed for a future based on your current paradigm of what you *thought* the future held. This practice assumes life is linear, and, based upon today, tomorrow will look a certain way. However, by the time the future arrives, many butterflies will have flapped their wings.

This is why it's more important for church leaders to remain flexible and daily strive to be sensitive to the Holy Spirit. My strategic plan is that, for the next ten years, I will daily put my faith in God, trust that he will direct my path, and be obedient to what the Spirit places on my heart.

Only God Knows

Life isn't always fair. It doesn't always make sense. Rarely does it follow *our* strategic plan. The life that we live doesn't occur in a linear fashion, but in a non-linear one. You may have an expectation that your life will take place day-by-day with incremental changes that will logically lead you to some outcome that you're striving for. The truth is, you have no clue what will happen from moment-to-moment in your life because life doesn't move along a logical, planned, and sequential path.

The comfort that you have is that God is in control of your life and has your steps laid out. All you have to do is wake up

Cairn Marker #1: A MIRAGE IN THE DESERT

every day, be sensitive to God's leading, and be obedient to placing your feet in the footprints he has already mapped out for you.[1] You must simply trust that he has a strategic plan for your life. From what I've read in the Bible and personally experienced, God—not being saddled to a logical path—can bring us to places that are unimaginable. Often, he does so in the most unlikely and unusual ways.

God's path for your life will take you through difficulties and trying circumstances which don't seem logical to you. It usually isn't what you had imagined that his will for you would be. You may endure hardships which feel like they're going to break you rather than be used to bless you. An all-familiar verse that we often turn to during these times is "'I say this because I know what I am planning for you,' says the Lord. 'I have good plans for you, not plans to hurt you. I will give you hope and a good future.'"[2]

When you go through times where you feel like giving up because of what you're going through, you must remind yourself that God has good plans for you and doesn't have plans to hurt you. He gives you hope and a good future. Whatever it is that you may go through, you will get through it. You will only get to see the beauty of what God has for you if we don't give up! Rather, you must continue to trust that the non-linear path he has planned for you to travel on will take you to a place that's better than where you could have ever imagined your linear, strategic plan taking you.

Hannah Hurnard beautifully depicts this scenario in her book, *Hinds' Feet on High Places*. At one point in the story, the crippled and deformed deer named Much-Afraid, who is being taken by the Good Shepherd to the High Places, turns a

---

1. "The steps of the God-pursuing ones follow firmly in the footsteps of the Lord, and God delights in every step they take to follow him" Psalms 37:23 (TPT).

2. Jeremiah 29:11 (NCV)

Soliloquy № 7

corner in the path. The direction of the path turns away from the mountains where the High Places were located and leads in the opposite direction through the desert.

"'I cannot go down there,' panted Much-Afraid, sick with shock and fear. 'He called me up to the High Places, and this is an absolute contradiction of all that he promised.'" After Much-Afraid pleads with the Good Shepherd over the apparent contradiction to the promise he made to her, the Good Shepherd replies to Much-Afraid: "It is not contradiction, only postponement for the best to become possible...Much-Afraid, do you love me enough to accept the postponement and the apparent contradiction of the promise, and to go down there with me into the desert?" Much-Afraid, in an act of complete submission, agrees to go with him into the wilderness which is in the opposite direction of the promise, and says, "Even if you cannot tell me why it has to be, I will go with you...for you have the right to choose for me anything that you please."

Towards the end of the book, when she finally arrives at the promised High Places, the Good Shepherd asks Much-Afraid (whose name he had changed to Grace-and-Glory) what she had learned. She said, "I learned that I must accept with joy all that you allowed to happen to me on the way and everything to which the path led me!" Then she said the most profound thing to the Shepherd:

> Every circumstance in life, no matter how crooked and distorted and ugly it appears to be, if it is reacted to in love and forgiveness and obedience to your will can be transformed. Therefore I begin to think, my Lord, you purposely allow us to be brought into contact with the bad and evil things that you want changed. Perhaps that is the very reason why we are here in this world, where sin and sorrow and suffering and evil abound, so that we may let

you teach us how to react to them, that out of them we can create lovely qualities to live forever. That is the only really satisfactory way of dealing with evil, not simply binding it so that it cannot work harm, but whenever possible overcoming it with good.

When you continue to follow the path that God has laid before you without giving up, the reward for doing so is disproportionately bigger than the effort you took to stay on that path despite the difficulties, frustrations, or lack of immediate reward or recognition.

CAIRN MARKER #2:
DESERT SAGE

The *Midrashim*, or "commentaries," are legendary expositions on the Old Testament that were written by ancient Rabbinical authorities. The Midrashim are mentioned twice in the Hebrew Bible. In 2 Chronicles 13:22, mention is made of "the rest of Abijah's accomplishments, his lifestyle and his memoirs are recorded in the Midrash of the Prophet Iddo" (ISV). Another reference is made in 2 Chronicles 23:27: "Records concerning his [Joash's] sons, the various statements rebuking him, and records of the reconstruction work on God's Temple are written in the Midrash of the Book of Kings" (ISV).

Rabbi Eliyahu Kitov, a Haredi Jew who studied Jewish history, its traditions, and customs, wrote a three-volume Midrashic commentary entitled *The Book of Our Heritage*. In it he captured some of the history passed down through the ages and taught by Jewish Rabbis for millennia. One of the stories he recorded was a traditional commentary that so beautifully frames the life of David. Although the following series of events, as recorded in Rabbi Kitov's work, aren't explicitly mentioned in Scripture, they are traditionally held to be true by Jewish scholars.

I encourage you to open your heart to the Spirit and your mind to the possibility of these events having actually occurred. Even if they had never actually happened, the story provides a powerful example of how life is not linear, attitude is everything, trusting and obeying God is essential even when the outcome is unknown, and experiencing disproportionately large blessings when compared to the effort invested and not giving up.

It all began with a woman named Ruth...

A Desert Rose

Ruth wasn't born a God-fearing Israelite, but a Moabite woman. Historically, many nations had mistreated Israel. This mistreatment brought the judgement of God upon them as a result. Jacob (whose name was later changed to Israel) had a brother named Esau, the father of the Edomites. The Edomites were too weak to come against Israel themselves, but they loved to take every opportunity to celebrate the success of other peoples who had done so.

Egypt was the first to enslave, persecute, and even kill all male Israelite babies two-years-old and under. The Lord instructed the Israelites, "Don't detest Edomites, since they are related to you. Don't detest Egyptians, either, because you were strangers in their land. Their grandchildren may participate in the assembly of the Lord." But, "No Ammonite or Moabite may enter the assembly of the Lord. Even to the tenth generation, none of them may enter the assembly of the Lord forever."[1] The reason God gave this command was because Ammon and

---

1. Deuteronomy 23:7-8 (ISV)

Moab had refused Israel food and drink after Israel had just come out of Egypt.

Moab had treated Israel even worse than Ammon did. "O my people, remember what Balak king of Moab devised..."[1] "They hired against you Balaam the son of Beor from Pethor of Mesopotamia, to curse you."[2] Balak, the king of Moab, had a grandson named Eglon who became the king of Moab.[3] According to rabbis in the Talmudic tradition, Ruth was one of Eglon's granddaughters.[4]

One of the characteristics of God is his lovingkindness, which was very seldom reflected by the Jews. The Moabites had been held accountable to God for not possessing or demonstrating lovingkindness to the Israelites. Ruth the Moabite, however, possessed an exceptionally rare quality of God's lovingkindness.

As the story goes in the book of Ruth, she was the daughter-in-law of Naomi. Naomi was from Bethlehem and an Israelite. After Naomi's husband and sons had died, Naomi and Ruth returned to Bethlehem in Israel. Ruth—being a Moabite—never imagined she would be anything other than a simple maidservant whose life would end after the death of Naomi. As the law stated, "No Ammonite or Moabite may enter the assembly of the Lord...forever."[5]

There didn't seem to be any differentiation between men and women when this command was given. Since the time that God had given the law, there had never been a need to question if there was a differentiation. The traditional telling of the story that Rabbi Kitov recorded identifies the first time that this issue

---

1. Micah 6:5
2. Deuteronomy 23:4
3. Judges 3:12
4. Talmud Sanhedrin, 105b
5. Deuteronomy 23:7-8 (ISV)

Soliloquy № 7

arose. It was in the case of the leaders of Israel discussing the request Boaz made to take Ruth as his wife in a Levirate marriage. Their conclusion was that this law only referred to the men of Ammon or Moab and did not include the women, for it wasn't acceptable for women to go out and provide those travelling through with provisions.

Therefore, it would be permissible for a *Moabitess* to enter the assembly of the Lord. However, in the midst of this uncertainty of this conclusion, the closer relative of Ruth's deceased husband, who had the first right to marry Ruth and redeem her, was reluctant to take her as his wife. He didn't want to jeopardize his own future in light of the law, and feared, "Lest I impair my own inheritance."[1] Boaz, being the next in line to redeem her, gladly accepted his role to marry her and raise up an heir for her deceased husband.

After Ruth had been allowed to join the assembly of Israel, the issue of allowing Ammonite or Moabite women to join in with the Israelites was put out of mind as the issue never had the need to be addressed again. However, there was always a measure of doubt that persisted in the minds of the leaders of Israel and their successors about the decision that was made to allow Ruth the Moabite woman to join the assembly.

Rabbi Kitov reveals in hindsight that this doubt was also a part of God's plan and held a secret reason that would only be illuminated at the right time when the light of the Messiah would be revealed. He writes, "The Mashiach [Messiah] was to first pass through stages of trepidation and fear. The path of the anointed king—David—was to be paved with two extremes: abysmal depths on one hand and Heavenly heights leading to the celestial throne on the other."

---

1. Ruth 4:6

Cairn Marker #2: DESERT SAGE

Paths in the Wilderness

The Greek philosopher Seneca once said, "It is a rough road that leads to the heights of greatness." Rabbi Kitov echoed this sentiment, stating that the path the anointed king would travel on would be one of both "grandeur and humility." Only God could have orchestrated the circumstances and given the leaders of Israel the discernment that would allow Ruth to marry Boaz to bring about the birth of the Messiah.

Boaz was the personification of grandeur. Ruth, however, scavenged for food to keep herself and Naomi alive. She was a marginalized member of society since she was a widow with no husband to provide for her, no children to care for her, *and* she was a Moabite convert to the assembly. She was the personification of humility.

Rabbi Kitov beautifully took this contrast of grandeur and humility found in Boaz and Ruth and wrote, "The Holy One, blessed is He, who knows the secrets of the heart, perceived the concurrent concealed aspects of their characters—the humility of Boaz and the grandeur of Ruth." However, contained in Boaz's grandeur was the embodiment of humility, and within Ruth's humility lay the promise of grandeur. For when Boaz and Ruth were married, David would become their direct descendent who would be the king of Israel from whom Jesus would descend—the embodiment of both grandeur and humility!

Three generations separated Ruth from David, her great-grandson. Boaz and Ruth had a son named Obed, and Obed's son was Jesse. The seventh son of Jesse was David. Hebrew tradition states that Obed was conceived the night of Boaz and Ruth's wedding, and that the next morning, the eighty-three-year-old Boaz was dead.[1]

While there were many who never doubted the accuracy of the decision made by the leaders that permitted Ruth the

---

1. Midrash Yalkut Shimoni, 608

Soliloquy № 7

Moabite to marry Boaz the Israelite, those who *did* doubt viewed Boaz's death as a punishment for having broken God's law of allowing a Moabite to join the assembly of the Lord. They likely confirmed this suspicion in their minds by recalling that Elimelech's sons were both killed—by God, they would assume—because they had both married Moabite women. Ruth was one of them.

Naomi became the nurse of the baby Obed, and the women of the neighborhood gave the baby his name.[1] Why did neighborhood women give the baby his name and not his parents which is the Jewish custom? And why would Naomi become Obed's nurse? Answers to these questions could support the traditionally-held belief that Boaz died before the baby Obed was born, requiring Ruth to once again spend her time supplying food for the family. When the women of the neighborhood came to celebrate over the baby's birth, they didn't offer their words to Ruth, but to Naomi. Perhaps as they said, "A son has been born to Naomi,"[2] it was so that Obed might be seen as an Israelite male and not a Moabite male who would not be allowed into Israel.

Black Sheep

Jewish tradition holds that the reason for the book of Ruth's inclusion in the Bible is to show that the Kingdom of Heaven can only be attained through suffering and affliction, which was the path that both Ruth and David walked. While Ruth suffered greatly in the loss of her husband(s), indenturing herself to care for the needs of her mother-in-law in humility by trusting her life to the lovingkindness of others (which was scarce at that

---

1. Ruth 4:16-17

2. Ruth 4:17

Cairn Marker #2: DESERT SAGE

time—especially with her being a Moabite living among the Israelites), David likely suffered even greater than she did.

David would write in a Psalm:

> Save me, O God! For the waters come up to my neck. I sink in deep mire, where there is no foothold; I have come into deep waters, and the flood sweeps over me. I am weary with my crying out; my throat is parched. My eyes grow dim with waiting for God. More in number than the hairs of my head are those who hate me without a cause; mighty are those who would destroy me, those who attack me with lies. What I did not steal must I now restore?... For it is for your sake that I have borne reproach, that dishonor has covered my face. I have become a stranger to my brothers, an alien to my mother's sons. For zeal for your house has consumed me,[1] and the reproaches of those who reproach you have fallen on me. When I wept and humbled my soul with fasting, it became my reproach.

---

1 While this portion is typically read from the personal perspective of David, being understood to say "I am consumed with zeal for your house," the correct interpretation may be "In the zeal that others have for possessing your house I have been consumed by them." A modern English translation of the Old Testament based on traditional Jewish sources called *The Living Nach* reads, "Out of envy for Your House, they ravaged me; the disgraces of those who revile You have fallen on me..." In light of the second part of this verse, this second interpretation appears to be more consistent in keeping with David's lamenting over the fact that he has been forsaken by his family as they purposefully neglected to call for him when Samuel came to Jesse to anoint one of his sons as king over God's people and had left him out in the wilderness. David's brothers, who despised him already, would be zealous for the opportunity of becoming the king of Israel as they were likely to view themselves as more qualified for the position (as you will soon discover why).

Soliloquy № 7

> When I made sackcloth my clothing, I became a byword to them. I am the talk of those who sit in the gate, and drunkards make songs about me... Reproaches have broken my heart, so that I am in despair. I looked for pity, but there was none, and for comforters, but I found none. They gave me poison for food, and for my thirst they gave me sour wine to drink.[1]

Why was David in such agony when he wrote this Psalm as a reflection on his circumstances? What could have happened in his life that would have him being shunned by his brothers, the leaders of Israel who sat at the gates of the city, and even had drunkards singing songs about a lowly shepherd-boy? It wasn't as if David was a high-profile celebrity that he should become the focus of the city's attention. David was even accused of stealing things and made to restore what he hadn't even stolen.

Probably the thing that would cause a person the most anguish is rejection by one's own family. When David wrote that he was a "stranger" he used the Hebrew word *muzar* which contains the same root word *zar* that is used in *mamzer*—"a child born from a stranger" (typically the result of an incestuous or adulterous relationship). He was expressing that, while he was of blood relation to his brothers, they estranged him as one who was not born from a legitimate relationship. Rabbi Kitov writes, "When they came in they saw him, when they left they saw him. The point had been reached wherein they could no longer abide in his presence. Can there be any greater anguish than this? What had David done to deserve this treatment?"

David had been born into the family of Jesse. The Talmud says Jesse was such an upright and blameless man that when he died, it wasn't because of any sin or flaw of his own, but

---

1. Psalms 69:1-4, 7-12, 20-21

because of the death decreed by the sin of Adam.[1] David's other brothers were all held in the same esteem as Jesse. Yet, when David had been born, this family of notoriety greeted his birth with contempt. Rabbi Shabbetai Kohen, in his commentary on Jewish law,[2] wrote that David wasn't allowed to eat with the rest of the family and was given a table in the corner to eat at alone. David was also assigned the task of shepherding his father's flocks in a remote area of the wilderness where bears and lions were in abundance. His brothers hoped that he would be killed while tending the flock alone. How could this be? What caused David to become the "black sheep" in his family?

Dark Nights

Rabbi Kitov writes that, because Jesse had walked in complete uprightness before the Lord, he feared in his old age that perhaps the leaders of Israel had made an error in their ruling to allow Boaz and Ruth (his grandparents) to marry which permitted a Moabite to enter into Israel. This thought troubled him as he pondered whether or not he was even fit to be a part of Israel himself. Jesse's life was a testimony to righteous living as were the lives of his sons.

Jesse's thoughts were troubled further in the fact that, if he were indeed part Moabite, he was married to a legitimate daughter of Israel. This would cause him to be guilty of breaking the law of God. Because of his fears, he decided to separate himself from his wife. (The Talmud states that the name of Jesse's wife was Nizbeth, the daughter of Adael.[3])

---

1. Talmud Shabbath, 55b
2. Siftei Kohen, 1646
3. Talmud Baba Batra, 91a

Jesse disclosed his dilemma to his six sons so that they would understand why he was separating himself from their mother.

After Jesse had been separated from Nizbeth for several years, he reasoned to himself that God still wanted the world to be populated, having given the command to Adam and Eve in Genesis. God had said it was not good for man to be alone. So, he took one of the Canaanite maidservants that was of his household to be his wife. The maidservant saw the anguish that plagued Nizbeth because of having to be separated from her husband, Jesse. She suggested to Nizbeth that they secretly switch places as Leah had done with Rachel.[1] When Jesse went in to sleep with the maidservant, he didn't know that she had switched places with Nizbeth.

Three months passed. As Jesse had disclosed the reason behind his separation to his sons, when they noticed that their mother was pregnant, they were indignant. They told their father she had been unfaithful to him and that she should be killed along with the unborn baby. Rather than allow them to do this, Jesse told his sons to let her birth the child so that they would remain blameless in not having taken the life of their mother and an unborn child. However, he said the baby should be born, and—just as a scapegoat which has the sins of the people placed upon it and is sent into the wilderness—become their servant and be abhorred by them. After all, Moab and ben-Ammi—the fathers of Moab and Ammon—were *mamzers* (as Jesse and his sons presumed the baby to be), and *mamzers* were not permitted to be admitted into the congregation of the Lord.

Kitov writes, "Yishai [Jesse] thought to prevent the child—David—from being accepted into the community of Israel in this manner (by establishing his status as an "abhorred servant") without having to publicize the fact that he was a *mamzer* [illegitimate child]." Meanwhile, Nizbeth decided she would forever take a vow of silence and carry the unbearable weight of

---

1. Genesis 29

Cairn Marker #2: DESERT SAGE

knowing that David *was* legitimate. She would have to watch in silence as he was mistreated by his brothers and forgotten by his father.

Jesse, considered to be one of the greatest men of his time, had the attention of everyone who lived in the city of Bethlehem. When he walked, his sons travelled behind him—all except for David whom they detested. His brothers would drive him away in contempt. The people, not knowing why Jesse and his sons kept their distance from David, would let their minds wander and fill in the blanks with their own narrative of things that weren't true about David. He literally became the scapegoat on which the people of Bethlehem cast their accusations. They could justify this behavior by rationalizing that if David's own family detested him, then by taking part in the harsh treatment of David they were blessing the house of Jesse.

David would be driven to the wilderness along with the sheep. When David "Looked for pity, but there was none, and for comforters, but I found none," the only one present was God, with whom David became well acquainted during his time of isolation.

Have you ever felt like this?

David was clueless as to why he was being treated the way that he was by everyone. There wasn't a single person who had compassion on David for what he was experiencing. He had no one to comfort him, encourage him, believe in him, be in community/relationship with him, or who would love him like family is supposed to love. Likely, the only time in his life that he experienced any of these things we count necessary for sanity and survival was during his early childhood. Before he was old enough to be sent out to tend the sheep, his mother would have undoubtedly lavished him with love as she nurtured him and raised him. As he grew up, he became aware that he was missing these things in his own life because he was able to see them in everyone else's lives but his own.

Soliloquy № 7

At times, there are circumstances you may encounter while following God's path for your life in ministry that cause you to feel the way David must have felt. The Latin words *circum* (which means "around") and *stance* (meaning "to stand") combine to describe the things that "stand around" you. These *circumstances* keep you from seeing what is on the other side of them.

You may not understand why you're being treated the way you are by your church "family" or by people that you minister to when you're serving them with love. You may be accused of doing things you haven't done or would never do; of being some kind of person that you aren't. You may feel as though you have purposely been placed in an environment with the intent for it to destroy you. You may be lonely, without support, and have no one who seems to care about your situation. David wrote, "I am like a lonely sparrow on the housetop."[1] Ever felt like that?

Only God knows what is on the other side of your circumstances. There's no way of knowing how long you may be in the wilderness, fighting bears and lions alone with no one to notice, help, or celebrate your accomplishments. You may be in a position where you view your task as unimportant, beneath you, and getting you nowhere in life.

These are the "make-or break" moments in your life and ministry. When you encounter these moments, you have two options: (1) You can pull out. Quit. Nobody would have missed David, and he could have gone somewhere else where his past was unknown and where he could start fresh. Or (2) You can press in. Engage. David chose to take that season of his life to fixate on God. Rabbi Kitov writes:

> How many are the obstacles and stumbling blocks in the way of a person who seeks to cleave to God when he is in the company of his

---

1. Psalms 102:7

fellowman! Distractions stand in one's way and the eyes of others watching are damaging to he who seeks to draw close to God. Man is constantly distracted—either by the love of those who are fond of him or by the enmity of those who hate him. When does he have the time to study the statutes of God and know His laws so that he might cleave to Him?

You can either hate your time in the wilderness or come to view it as a gift from God. While this is easy for me to write (and easy for you to read), it's exceedingly difficult for the both of us to do when we're in a wilderness. Hal Donaldson, founder of Convoy of Hope once said that when you go through difficult times in your life, rather than asking God, "Why?" (as in, "Why are you allowing me to go through this?") and seeking to understand God's reasoning, ask God, "What?" (as in, "What are you wanting to teach me and do in me through this?") and seek to know God more. Again, David would write, "It is good for me that I was afflicted, that I might learn your statutes."[1]

This is important: **What is happening *in* you is more important than what is happening *to* you.** Your character is being formed as you are alone in the wilderness with God.

This story of David that's been passed down in the Midrashim could have easily served as the inspiration for the children's story *The Ugly Duckling* written by Hans Christian Anderson. For those not familiar with the story, it's about a young swan that was hatched in a duck's nest. The baby swan was marked as "different" and was not seen as a beautiful swanling, but rather as an "ugly duckling." The ugly duckling was abused and humiliated by his sibling ducklings which had also hatched in the nest. The way they treated him made him feel worthless. This caused the ugly duckling to run away from his

---

1. Psalms 119:71

Soliloquy № 7

humiliation and sufferings. When he returned a year later, he had become a beautiful swan, and he was finally able to experience the happiness he never had as an ugly duckling.

Unbeknownst to David, he, too, was a beautiful baby swan who had been growing up in a dynasty of ducks. After spending time away in the wilderness with God, he developed into a beautiful swan. On this day, David was about to discover the destiny God had been planning for him for generations. David wrote, "Crying may last for a night, but joy comes in the morning."[1]

Now imagine this scenario with me.

David has spent the night with his sheep in a remote and dangerous part of the wilderness. He's cried himself to sleep—not because he's afraid, but because he's broken. He's been pouring his heart out to God, and the sun is breaking over the horizon in the east. The bleating of sheep begins to sporadically break the monotony of the crickets that have relentlessly chirped through the night. For David, the dawning day will be just another day like the day before.

Solitude.

In the forefront of his mind, he has a dependence upon his growing relationship with God. But in the back of his mind, he has a nagging sense of rejection, abandonment, and worthlessness. He will spend another day alone with smelly sheep under a hot sun with no one to take notice of him while he faithfully executes the responsibility of tending sheep entrusted to him by his father. He has no idea that on this day, God has prepared a Black Swan event for him.

Beautiful Sunrises

"Fill your horn with oil and go. I will send you to Jesse the Bethlehemite, for <u>I have provided for myself a king</u> among his

---

1. Psalms 30:5 (NCV)

sons...The elders of the city came to meet him trembling..."[1] The leaders of Bethlehem knew that Samuel, being a prophet of God, must have come to fulfill an important mission. Because David hadn't quit trusting in God, had been faithful and obedient to what he was entrusted with—despite his circumstances, and had allowed his character to be formed in the midst of suffering, God had been in the process of preparing something disproportionately wonderful for David all along. God had been forming David to become the king of Israel. And only God knew that this was what he was up to the whole time.

Samuel had been instructed to invite Jesse for a sacrifice unto God. Because God hadn't told Samuel which of Jesse's sons he was going to anoint as king, Samuel told Jesse to bring his sons who were with him to the sacrifice (Samuel must have assumed that all of Jesse's sons were present), and then Samuel consecrated Jesse's sons.[2] However, David wasn't with his brothers when Samuel invited Jesse and his sons who were with him to come to the sacrifice.

Now, pay close attention.

1 Chronicles 2:13-16 lists the names of the *seven* sons of Jesse in the order they were born, with David being listed as the seventh son.[3] Then, in 1 Samuel 16:10 we are told that "Jesse made seven *of his sons*[4] pass before Samuel."

Something doesn't add up.

If Jesse made seven of his sons pass before Samuel, how could David still be out in the field with the sheep? The only way that this is possible is if Jesse had at least eight sons. In

---

1. 1 Samuel 16:1, 4

2. 1 Samuel 16:5

3. "Jesse fathered Eliab his firstborn, Abinidab the second, Shimea the third, Nethanel the fourth, Raddai the fifth, Ozzem the sixth, David the seventh" (1 Chronicles 2:13-16).

4. The use of the word "of" indicates that there were more sons, and that all of Jesse's sons were not present to pass before Samuel.

what seems like a contradiction, 1 Samuel 17:12 says that Jesse did in fact have *eight* sons.[1] The name of the eighth son that was with Jesse was Elihu. He's not listed in 1 Chronicles 2:13-16 where the seven sons of Jesse are listed, most likely because Elihu was not yet born. However, he's mentioned in the listing of the leaders of the tribes of Israel in 1 Chronicles 27:18.[2] Rabbi Kitov states that tradition holds that Elihu was younger than David and was born to Jesse by another wife other than Nizbeth, possibly the Canaanite maidservant he had married.

Samuel, not sensing that any of the sons Jesse made to pass before him was God's chosen, had to ask Jesse, "Are all your sons here?"[3] Jesse replied, "There remains the **youngest**, but behold, he is keeping the sheep." Because David was tending the sheep, he was not with all of his brothers when Samuel invited Jesse and his sons (who were with him) to sacrifice to the Lord.

Now if you are like me, you are asking yourself, "But didn't Jesse reply that his *youngest* son—David—remained in the field?" To address this question, let's look at the original language that was used for the word "youngest." Jesse used the Hebrew word *qatan*, which means "insignificant" or "unimportant." This word is used again in 1 Samuel 17:14 when it says that David was the youngest—*qatan*—that is, "insignificant." David couldn't be the youngest son of Jesse, even though he was named as the seventh son of Jesse in 1 Chronicles 2:16, because Jesse made seven of his sons pass before Samuel while David was still in the field tending the sheep. Remember, 1 Samuel 17:12 states that Jesse had eight sons.

Even though Elihu was younger than David, he (Elihu) seemed to be more important to Jesse than David because

---

1. "Now David was the son of an Ephrathite of Bethlehem in Judah, named Jesse, **who had eight sons**" (1 Samuel 17:12) [emphasis added].

2. "for Judah, Elihu, one of David's brothers" (1 Chronicles 27:18).

3. 1 Samuel 16:11

he was present at the sacrifice and David wasn't. Normally, it was the youngest child who was given the lowly job of tending sheep. However, David was "insignificant" to Jesse (even though he was older than Elihu) because he was the one tending the sheep. Jesse never thought about sending for David to come to the sacrifice, because he didn't view David as *his* son. Nizbeth had never revealed her secret to Jesse.

The Complete Jewish Bible states that David was red headed[1] and, as far as Jesse knew, technically his stepchild. David was certainly being treated like (according to every imaginable definition of the term) a "red-headed stepchild." This could very well be the etymology of this phrase as no one seems to know for sure where it came from and how it came to describe a person who is neglected, mistreated, and unwanted.

Black Swans

"Then Samuel took the horn of oil and anointed him in the midst of his brothers."[2] In this moment, David became the anointed king of Israel. A Black Swan event—possessing a disproportionate blessing which paled in comparison with the isolation, rejection, and abandonment David had experienced for his entire life—had just happened to him. He had been rewarded for being faithful and allowing God to "make for Himself a king" for his people. David was "a man after God's own heart."[3] David's relationship with God was the only real relationship that he had ever known. His time tending sheep in the

---

1. "He sent and brought him in. With ruddy cheeks, *red hair* and bright eyes, he was a good-looking fellow" 1 Samuel 16:12 (CJB) [emphasis added].

2. 1 Samuel 16:13

3. 1 Samuel 13:14

Soliloquy № 7

wilderness gave God the opportunity to make a king that would be in relationship with him and after his heart.

And now, his moment had come.

After God's Spirit had been taken from Saul, the current king of Israel, and he was being tormented by a demon, he needed someone who could skillfully play music to comfort him in his torment. Where once people accused David of crimes he didn't commit and drunkards sang songs about him, he was now described in a totally different way. "Behold, I have seen a son of Jesse the Bethlehemite, who is skillful in playing, a man of valor, a man of war, prudent in speech, and a man of good presence, and the Lord is with him."[1] Like Giovanni in *The Tartar Steppe* who spent his entire life on the edge of the wilderness, faithfully keeping watch for an attack by an enemy who had never been seen and then finally experiencing that event, God had been preparing David for a moment that he had planned all along. David had no idea he would be king of Israel or that it could even be possible.

YOUR CURRENT WILDERNESS

I wonder how many parallels between the life of David and the life of Jesus can you draw from this story? Rabbi Kitov said that the Messiah would walk the same path to becoming king that David had paved. For example, Psalm 69:21 says, "They gave me [David] also gall for my food; and in my thirst they gave me vinegar to drink," while Matthew 27:34 says, "They gave him [Jesus] vinegar to drink mixed with gall."

Throughout Matthew's Gospel Jesus was called the *son of David*.[2] He, too, was familiar with loneliness, rejection and abandonment while walking the path God had laid out for him

---

1. 1 Samuel 16:18

2. Matthew 1:1, 15:22, 20:31, 22:42

as he was being prepared to establish his throne in heaven and in the hearts of men. In many regards, the idiom, "Like father, like son" holds true in the life of Jesus.

You, also, must not forget that the life you are living is your wilderness experience where God is preparing you to take positions in heaven where you will rule and reign with him. "If we have died with Him, we will also live with Him; if we endure, we will also reign with Him."[1] A time is coming when you will be called out of your wilderness where you are caring for the flocks that the Father has entrusted to you, and you are anointed to rule and reign with Christ. He's preparing you in your wilderness. It's in your wilderness that you must worship God for who he is, and, as David did, cry out to God, learn to hear his voice and be after his heart.

Your life on earth is an internship that's preparing you for what he will have you do in heaven. "Do you not know that the saints will judge the world? And if the world is to be judged by you, are you incompetent to try trivial cases? Do you not know that we are to judge angels? How much more, then, matters pertaining to this life?"[2]

So, don't give up! If God has called you to the work that you are currently doing, stay with what he's called you to do and don't let the worldly expectation of linearity and fairness discourage you from persevering. The path that you are walking along with Christ doesn't travel in a linear fashion; rather it is non-linear and often, full of unfairness. This makes the rewards of your continued efforts bigger in proportion to the efforts you put forth. It's not what you *do* that makes you as rare as a black swan but who you *are becoming* that makes you rare as you go through your life—no matter how difficult. Hebrews 10:32-38 (NLT) says:

---

1. 2 Timothy 2:11

2. 1 Corinthians 6:2-4

Soliloquy № 7

> Think back on those early days when you first learned about Christ. Remember how you remained faithful even though it meant terrible suffering. Sometimes you were exposed to public ridicule and were beaten, and sometimes you helped others who were suffering the same things. You suffered along with those who were thrown into jail, and when all you owned was taken from you, you accepted it with joy. You knew there were better things waiting for you that would last forever.
>
> So, do not throw away this confident trust in the Lord. Remember the great reward it brings you! Patient endurance is what you need now, so that you will continue to do God's will. Then you will receive all that he has promised. "For in just a little while, the Coming One will come and not delay. And my righteous ones will live by faith. But I will take no pleasure in anyone who turns away."

While you may be encountering the most challenging time in your life that you've faced to-date, you don't know what Black Swan event may be waiting for you to encounter tomorrow. It may be weeks, months, or years before you get to see what God has been preparing *you* for and preparing *for* you. You may not like reading the next statement, but you may not see the Black Swan event in your lifetime as you don't know God's plans. Your Black Swan moment may be when you step into the clouds of heaven and hear the King say to you—as Giovanni heard the king in his daydream say to him after persevering in battle, "Well done!" The bottom line is that you can't give up in the process of what God is making you to become.

***

Cairn Marker #2: DESERT SAGE

There is a saying: "It was the last straw that broke the camel's back." It connotes that we don't know the point at which just one more thing—no matter how small or insignificant—will create an unpredictably large and sudden reaction. I can't think of an idiom that's the opposite of this—perhaps because it's easier to see limitations than it is to see what's possible. So, here's my attempt at creating one: "*What may appear from a distance to be a black sheep may actually turn out to be a Black Swan.*" Don't fall prey to the cognitive bias that would have you making choices today that affects your future, but are based strictly on your past/present circumstances. Stay on your path, trust God, and don't give up.

Admonishment #4: Watch for where God has you going and stay on the path that he has put you on. Trust that whatever circumstances you encounter on the path God has you on are planned and on purpose. God will reward you if you don't give up!

Questions:

- Since Black Swan events seem so very rare in our lives, in what ways does this bias show up in your life and most often affect you?
- Are there any instances that you can reflect on or can see how you allowed this bias to keep you from a reward that was bigger than the pain of the circumstances you were experiencing?
- How have you tried to make predictions about your life based on past occurrences?
- Have you ever thought that the Good Shepherd was making a mistake by leading you into the desert rather than directly into green pastures, and if so, did you follow his leading, or do what *you* thought was best?

Soliloquy № 7

- Do you have a strategic plan for your life and/or ministry that is forecast into the future?
- Are you willing to daily follow God in faith and alter your plan rather than keep following what *you* think the plan is supposed to be?
- Have you wanted to give up and quit what God has you doing because of your circumstances? How would that change things? What *could* happen if you don't give up and stick to the path?

"Don't allow yourself to be sidetracked for even a moment or take the detour that leads to darkness."

Proverbs 4:27 (TPT)

Five

ALTOGETHER SEPARATE:
Deviating from the Standard & the Conformity Bias

> *"It is easy in the world to live after the world's opinion; it is easy in solitude to live after our own; but the great man is he who in the midst of the crowd keeps with perfect sweetness the independence of solitude."*
>
> —Ralph Waldo Emerson, *Self-Reliance*

AUGUST LANDMESSER

On June 13, 1936, the workers at the Blohm & Voss Shipyard in Hamburg, Germany had assembled for the launching ceremony of a naval ship they had built called the *Horst Wessel*. The ship was used to train cadets for the German Navy until 1939 when it was decommissioned at the onset of World War II. After the war, ownership was transferred to the United States on May 15, 1946. It was then commissioned into the United States Coast Guard as the *USCGC Eagle*. Today, the ship is still in active service by the United States Coast Guard Academy in New London, Connecticut. It's now used to

Soliloquy № 7

provide at-sea leadership and professional development experiences for their future officers.

Attending the ship's launching ceremony in 1936 was the German Fuhrer, Adolf Hitler. As the newly-built ship was being launched, all the workers in the shipyard raised their right arm for the "Hitler-Gruss." While this scene was unfolding, a photograph was taken. Upon close inspection of the photo, you can notice that one lone individual in the sea of faces didn't have his arm raised in salute.

No one may ever know who took the photograph or what it might have been used for, but fifty-five years later, the photograph appeared in the March 22, 1991 edition of the German newspaper, *Die Ziet*. A woman by the name of Irene Eckler made an amazing discovery when she saw the picture in the newspaper. She identified the individual whose arm was not raised in salute as her father, August Landmesser.

Photo of August Landmesser that appeared in the newspaper, "Die Ziet"

World War I had devastated the German economy. Unemployment was rampant under the reining Weimar government. This enabled the Nazi Party to come into power by supplying jobs for those who were members of their political party. Many Germans joined the Nazi Party for survival. Landmesser didn't subscribe to Hitler's position regarding racial purity, but he joined the Nazi party in hopes that it would enable him to get a job.

In October of 1934, Landmesser met a girl named Irma Eckler. The two fell in love and made plans to marry in August of the following year. They went to the registry office to set their wedding plans in motion, but their wedding was denied because Irma was a Jew. A document entitled *The Law for the Protection of German Blood and German Honour* stated,

> § 1 (1) Marriages between Jews and subjects of German or kindred blood are forbidden. Marriages nevertheless concluded are invalid, even if they are concluded abroad to circumvent this law.

This law was set to take effect on September 15, 1935. It wouldn't be in effect until one month after their wedding was to take place, but they were still denied permission to marry. While the law might have prevented the two from getting married, it didn't keep them out of one another's arms. On October 29, 1935, their daughter, Ingrid, was born.

This created yet another problem. Article 2.1 of *The Law for the Protection of German Blood and German Honour* further stated,

> § 2 (1) Extramarital relations between Jews and subjects of the state of Germany or related blood are forbidden.

August and Irma had a child out of marriage. This action alone would have been enough to get Landmesser ousted from the Nazi party, but the two remained together, unmarried, but not

Soliloquy № 7

without consequence. For two years, August Landmesser was subjected to humiliation and was constantly fearful for his life. So, in 1937, he and his family decided to leave Germany. They were caught trying to cross the border into Denmark, and August was accused of "dishonoring the race." The court issued them both a warning which said that if he were to dishonor the German race again, Landmesser would be imprisoned. Unfortunately, Irma was pregnant with their second daughter when this warning was given.

Landmesser would find himself in and out of prison as he struggled to be with the woman he loved and their children. Ultimately, the law would overpower their will to be together. August was sentenced to two-and-a-half years of imprisonment and sent to Börgermoor Prison Camp I in Emsland, Germany. At the same time, the love of his life, the Jewish girl named Irma Eckler—or as the Germans would come to know her, KZ-928/574—was arrested three days later. Irma was sent to the Ravensbrück concentration camp. From there, she was transported to the Bernburg Killing Facility (the Euthanasia Centre at Bernburg) where she was murdered on April 28, 1942 in a gas chamber along with one thousand four hundred other Jewish women.

August Landmesser was released from prison camp on January 19, 1941. While it was obviously impossible for him to visit Irma in a concentration camp, he did manage to visit his daughters during the time he was working with a moving company. In 1944, he was drafted into a battalion— "Bewährungs bataillon XIX / 999" (Probation Battalion) as it was called— made up of ex-convicted criminals, political dissenters, and others who were considered unfit for society. They were esteemed about as highly as the Jews were, and they were made to wear a red triangle as the only insignia on their uniform. The triangle held an ironic semblance to the Star of David that the Jews were forced to wear on the outside of their clothing. August died in battle on October 17, 1944, fighting for a cause that he didn't believe in and that had kept him from living a life of happiness with the woman he loved.

Although the photograph had been taken in 1936, years before the tragic death of the love of his life, the German purity laws were already being established which denied him his desire to marry Irma and to be a father to their children. While the Nazi Party might have provided Landmesser with a job, they had stripped him of his family. Is there any wonder why this man refused to salute Hitler along with everyone else? It was clear from the photograph that the one thing the Nazi Party could *not* do was force Landmesser to conform his beliefs and behavior to that of the Nazi Party.

Unconquerable

There are moments when we're forced to search ourselves for what we really believe—for the values of which we will hold fast. That which is truly valuable can't be taken away from us or be altered in any way. It dwells inside of us and lies solely within our control. Happiness and satisfaction will never be reached until we discover who we are as individuals, are at peace with ourselves, and are fulfilling the purpose for which God has created us. "Self-contentment," said the first-century philosopher Seneca in *Letters from a Stoic*, "is the line we draw as the boundary for our happiness."

A story about a fourth-century Greek philosopher named Stilbo illustrates this beautifully. Demetrius, a Macedonian military powerhouse who would become king of Macedon, captured Stilbo's hometown. In the attack, Stilbo lost his wife and children. When Demetrius scoffingly asked him if he had lost anything, Stilbo replied, "I have all my valuables with me. I have lost nothing. All my possessions are with me." This reply caused Demetrius to wonder if he had won a victory at all.

Soliloquy № 7

What Stilbo was insinuating was that there are some things of value that can never be taken away. Those "things" are the beliefs, values, character traits, and sense of purpose that others can't remove from us. These moral fibers of our being are not a loose thread that can be easily unraveled without our consent. Those things can only be relinquished by one's self. Because of this, Seneca said that it was easier to conquer a whole people group rather than a single man.

When we're confident of who we are, what we believe, what we're capable of, and what we have been called to do, we have the power to keep our position of self-assurance. Our certainty of these things serves as the final authority for our decisions and our actions. The temptation to redraw our boundaries to accommodate or imitate those of another is diminished. We then become unconquerable.

CONFORMITY BIAS

Vladmir Nesov defines the *Conformity bias* as "a tendency to behave similarly to the others in a group, even if doing so goes against your own judgment." The Conformity bias explains why Landmesser made the decision to join the Nazi Party. While he didn't agree with the policies that the Nazi Party was promoting, it was easier to "join the party" than it was to act on his individual beliefs. His survival depended on this decision.

Conformity itself is a part of being human. We are social beings designed to interact with one another. Expectations for cooperation are established by either having others force those expectations upon us directly or by intuitively discovering them ourselves through our interactions with others. By cooperating with others, we meet less resistance.

As we are creatures of comfort, we naturally align our behavior with those around us because we have discovered it's easier to "go with the flow" than it is to "go against the grain."

In fact, social disapproval triggers the danger circuits of our brain which causes negative emotional reactions in response to the stress that stems from these circuits being activated.

When our actions are aligned with those around us, we don't have to spend the extra energy required to support our nonconformity. We've learned that we experience a lot less stress by merely observing the cues of the various cultures we find ourselves moving in and out of throughout the day; synchronizing our actions and behaviors with the people who are a part of those various cultures. It doesn't mean that, by conforming to the expected behaviors of the group, we enjoy doing whatever it is everybody else is doing or even agree with why they are doing it. Without being aware, we may be following the crowd as a survival instinct and because we enjoy the physiological comfort that conformity provides.

If you live in a Western culture such as the United States, the idea of "rugged individualism" and operating independently from others around you have permeated your worldview. We take pride in the freedom we have to live life as an independent member of society and make our own choices, including the ability to express our individuality and our uniqueness. This is often exhibited through our clothing style choices, our music preferences, our hairstyles, and the décor in our homes and offices. While we may choose to express our individuality in an effort to be somewhat "different" from everyone else, we unconsciously are comparing ourselves to those around us to determine if our choices are conforming with theirs.

In a futile effort to intentionally break free from conforming to the expectations of a group, we may *unintentionally* look for acceptance of our nonconformity by seeking to unite with others with whom we find similarity in behavior or agreement with in our beliefs. What we end up doing is merely exchanging conformity norms with another group of people. When everyone is doing something the same, it's human nature to want to be

Soliloquy № 7

noticed as an individual and not just be a face in the crowd. In this way we are "individual nonconformists."

We're social creatures, however, and have a need to belong to a group. This need will often have us adopt the practices of the group with which we are associating. We either conform to the group at-large, or we must decide to break from the group to express our individual beliefs. We may go along with the crowd until we feel we must be true to ourselves, but because of our innate need to live in harmony with others, we simply end up conforming to other nonconformists. There are very few people who can completely break free from group conformity and completely abandon themselves to their individual ideas.

We can all see problems and issues associated with conforming to a group's norms. It's also natural to feel the desire to break free from the constraints of group conformity and reject the norms of the group. By doing so, we believe that we'll be free to express our independence, creating and following our own path. However, while it may appear that nonconformity is the solution, the only way for our independence to survive is to align with another group and work together with them.

It's one thing to see the need to break away from a group's norms and strike out on our own. For those who do, they usually suffer the consequences of nonconformity. For example, a motorist who breaks from the group norm of driving on the right-hand side of the road and decides to drive on the left-hand side of the road would cause injury to themselves and to others.

It's quite another thing to see the need for breaking away from a group's norms, identifying a better belief or behavior, and searching out others who have done the same. In this way, the problem of conformity to a group becomes the solution. So, it would appear that the group becomes the source of both conformity and rebellion.

ANCHORED

Once, when Seneca was asked what it was particularly that one should avoid, it was his opinion that one should avoid a mass crowd because of the risk associated with being with gatherings of people. He indicated that he never came back from being around a crowd with the same moral character that he had before he was with a crowd. It seemed to Seneca that he would arrive at a settled place in his thoughts and beliefs, but after associating with the crowd, the innate sociological factor to conform to a group that lies inside all of us would end up causing him to deviate from the internal peace at which he had arrived beforehand.

Seneca perceived that no matter how firm the resolve of an individual might be to *not* conform, the instinctive nature of being human—wired to observe informational cues of what's going on in a given context as well as normative cues of established beliefs and behavior of others around us—embodies a very strong pressure to align our own behavior and beliefs to the expectations of the group. He says in his writings of *Letters from a Stoic*:

> When a mind is impressionable and has none too firm a hold on what is right, it must be rescued from the crowd: it is so easy for it to go over to the majority. A Socrates, a Cato or a Laelius might have been shaken in his principles by a multitude of people different from himself: such is the measure of the inability of any of us, even as we perfect our personality's adjustment, to withstand the onset of vices when they come with such a mighty following.

It's impractical to avoid crowds just to keep from being influenced by the norms of groups in which we might find ourselves. While we may try to form our individual beliefs and behaviors on our own, the beliefs and behaviors of the people we surround ourselves with will shape us. Likewise, we're not always able to choose which groups of people we will or will not associate with, or choose the individuals that make up those groups. Given these realities, the only thing we can control when we are with a crowd is how we choose to behave based on our beliefs. This means we must spend as much or more time observing ourselves as we do those around us. Private introspection *and* public observation are essential to making good decisions as to whether we will conform, and how we will conform.

When it comes to conformity, a core issue that requires self-examination is motive. One of the motives for nonconformity may be the need for attention. An individual who doesn't conform to a group gains the attention of both those who may also be contemplating nonconformity to the group as well as those individuals who are conforming to the group. Some people crave the attention that nonconformity can bring them. It may be that they don't necessarily disagree with the group's norms; they just need the attention that comes with being different.

Another motive for nonconformity may be the individual's need for change. Perhaps the group's norms are no longer effective or relevant to the individual. Nonconformists may desire to work together with others for the greater good, but perhaps they're discontent with merely conforming to a group whose methodologies of achieving that greater good are irrelevant and/or ineffective. To the nonconformist, this type of group may appear mindless and dogmatic—doing things just because it has always been done a particular way. To the nonconformist, the group doesn't seem to notice that what they're doing or how they're doing it isn't working and is no longer relevant. Rather than spend the energy of trying to change the entire group, the nonconformist strikes out on their own.

Altogether Separate: Deviating from the Standard & the Conformity Bias

A third motive for nonconformity may be that of wanting to achieve the success that others who have broken from group conformity are experiencing. Embracing this motive can entangle a nonconformist in another bias called the *Prestige bias*. This bias occurs when you observe other nonconformists who are successful, study their behaviors and beliefs which don't conform to those of the dominant group's, and then adopt those beliefs and behaviors as one's own. This gives the individual who is acting under the influence of the Prestige bias the feeling that they, too, will experience the same success and be viewed by others as successful.

Like the Conformity bias, the Prestige bias serves as both a blessing and a curse. It's a blessing when obsolete practices, faulty beliefs, and ineffective methods are identified. Breaking from conformity to these types of toxic norms produces positive and effective changes and results. Other people are then also able to take notice of the ineffectiveness of a group, see the effectiveness in the actions and behavior of a nonconformist to that group, and then begin to replicate new ways of thinking and doing things.

Ironically, the Conformity bias steps in and takes over again as the practices of the nonconformists become more widely adopted and conformity occurs. The Prestige bias then becomes a curse. As the beliefs and behaviors of successful nonconformists are observed, they then begin to be emulated without the consideration of whether those beliefs and behaviors are actually beneficial to their group. Adopting these may produce successful results in the immediate, but they haven't been proven to actually be effective or beneficial in the long run.

Soliloquy № 7

Nebuchadnezzar's Golden Statu[t]e

The Bible tells the story of King Nebuchadnezzar who built a statue of himself.[1] The king summoned the leaders, officials, and those who were in authority within his province, to come to the dedication of the statue. Upon their arrival, an order was given to these key individuals that when music began to play, they were to bow down and worship the statue. Whoever did not would immediately be made an example of by being thrown into a furnace and burned alive.

There are a few interesting things to take note of in this story. First, the most influential and notable leaders from the region were called to attend the dedication. They represented numerous nations which included the people of Israel.

Did you ever notice that only *leaders* were summoned—not the people whom they were responsible for governing? There's a key truth that can be derived from this: **leaders are targets**. The king only summoned those who were in leadership over the people to attend the dedication because those whom they led would follow their example. The lesson here for leaders today is that **the testing of a leader's boundaries establishes the perimeters of conformity for the people they lead**. In other words, people "follow the leader." What's permissive in a leader's life will become permissive in the lives of those who follow them. The boundary lines of behavior and belief that leaders draw from will become the models and the inspiration that those they lead will draw from to establish their own boundaries.

Upon their arrival, the leaders saw the magnitude of the statue and all the pomp and circumstance of the occasion. The statue was the most extraordinary one that had ever been built. Other statues had been constructed, but none before were as big and breathtaking as this one. They were also greeted with a

---

1. Daniel 3

surprise by being given instructions to bow down and worship the statue when the music began to play. If they didn't, they would be "fired." No time was given for the leaders to consider the proposal before deciding. The command was simply given, and then the music began to play. Each leader had to instantly decide whether to conform to the expectation, regardless if they agreed with it or not. They immediately had to determine where the limits to their acceptance of the king's authority lay in each of their own lives.

While dwelling in Palestine, Israel's leaders had ceased to worship the One True God and had led the people into idol worship. They saw no problem in bowing down to worship idols as Moses said they would do.[1] In Daniel 3, the leaders were required to publicly declare their acceptance of King Nebuchadnezzar's authority by bowing before the golden statue. For Shadrach, Meshach, and Abednego, their decision would be more than merely a personal one. They knew they were responsible for leading the Jewish people who were watching to see what their decision would be. They had to immediately determine where the limits to their acceptance of the king's authority lay in each of their own lives.

Another interesting fact is that the sanction for nonconformity wasn't announced until the time that all the leaders had gathered for the dedication ceremony. The king himself called upon the leaders to assemble for the dedication of the statue on the plain of Dura in the province of Babylon. No agenda items had been sent out for review or consideration before the meeting. The king simply called for all the leadership to be a part of a ceremony.

Tests of our convictions often come with no warning. Leaders often find themselves in situations where they must make immediate decisions which will either influence or be influenced by their beliefs. There comes a moment when each

---

1. Deuteronomy 4:27-28

Soliloquy № 7

of us is forced to move beyond what we *think* to what we *believe*. When we're given the freedom to think without consequence, it's easy to declare what we would or wouldn't do; what we believe or what we don't believe. But when we're faced with a moment of decision, what we'll do in that moment must be influenced by what we believe. And what we believe must have already been firmly established. If not, what we do in that moment will be influenced by what others are doing and not by our own beliefs.

In another part of the country, Naaman, who was the "right hand man" of the king of Syria, had just been healed by God and had surrendered his life to him.[1] Now he was returning to resume his duties in service to his king. He explained to the prophet Elisha that he would be required to go with the king into the temple of Rimmon and bow before the god of the Syrians when the king went in to worship. Knowing that this action would place him in a compromising position, he asked for Elisha to pardon his actions in having to perform his duties in the service of the king. Elisha assured him that he could "Go in peace."

There is a difference between Naaman's situation and that of Shadrach, Meshach, and Abednego's. The Syrian king wasn't requiring Naaman to worship another god as the three Jewish leaders were being required to do by Nebuchadnezzar. Naaman, in his required duties, would only be accompanying his king into the house of Rimmon and bowing. He was not required to worship Rimmon. In each of these instances, both Naaman and the three Hebrews had fixed their gaze upon God and established him as their authority. This decision, made prior to being faced with the tests of their convictions, served as their anchor. Both Naaman and the three Hebrews would be in the crowd while others chose to worship another god, but they

---

1. 2 Kings 5:18-19

themselves would choose not to worship anyone or anything other than the One True God.

Jews who were watching Shadrach, Meshach, and Abednego weren't put into the position that these three leaders were. The crowd could talk about what they would or wouldn't do if they were put in the same position, but they didn't feel the pressure that these three young men were experiencing. The Jews in the crowd didn't have anything to lose by not bowing down like their three leaders did.

Shadrach, Meshach, and Abednego could, in their minds, make the rational decision to bow down and avoid being thrown into a furnace. Besides, the might and power of King Nebuchadnezzar was on display. They were looking at the biggest statue they had ever seen. The immense wealth of the king was there for all to see. The biggest names in leadership had been assembled in one place, and the influence that their positions afforded them by virtue of their connections, wisdom, and success must have placed pressure on the three Hebrew leaders to conform to the command of the king.

All these same aspects are a factor when we as church leaders today consider our natural tendency to conform to the values, beliefs, and behaviors of a group. Conforming our own lives to the beliefs and conduct of a group operates within the natural and rational realm of human intellect. Transforming our lives to *believe* and *conduct* the power of God operates in the supernatural and superrational[1] realm of divine faith. In leadership, it can be difficult to detect our bias towards group conformity while simultaneously striving to become leaders who want to one day hear the words, "Well done, good and faithful servant."

---

1. *Rational* is defined as being in accordance with reason and logic. *Superrational* then would be defined as reason and logic surpassing that of mortals.

Soliloquy № 7

DIDEROT UPGRADES

As we've discussed in chapter 1, success in church leadership is often not defined, and the means to achieving success are not clearly laid out. In a culture that has created an expectation that everything must "version up" in a never-ending progression of innovation, and that nothing should stay the same, we can begin to distance ourselves from those who adhere to "legacy" leadership practices and principles. Those methods seem to run too slow, are not equipped to handle upgraded leadership practices, and have ceased to capture the attention of others because they have become so commonplace. We've become mesmerized by "beta test bosses" who seem to be producing more results, are adapting their leadership capabilities to state-of-the-art patterns of action, and whose maverick methodologies have everyone else taking notice.

Without pausing to consider who *we* are, what *our* purpose is, and what God would have *us* to do, we may find ourselves wrestling with feelings of inadequacy. It may appear that everyone but us has upgraded their leadership protocols to conform to the dynamistic qualities and practices of the next generation leadership operating system.

This feeling closely resembles the *Diderot Effect*, named for the eighteenth-century French philosopher Denis Diderot. He had lived his entire life in poverty, and now his daughter was to be married. This meant that she needed a dowry in order to be wed, which Diderot couldn't afford. Fortunately, the Empress of Russia (Catherine the Great) offered him more than enough money in exchange for his library. He was the co-founder and writer of one of the most exhaustive encyclopedias of the day called the *Encyclopédie*, and he was extremely well-read.

With the leftover proceeds from the sale, Diderot bought for himself a new scarlet robe. To him, it was so beautiful that he became discontented with the rest of his humble possessions. He would later write an essay entitled *Regrets for My*

Old Dressing Gown that there was "no more coordination, no more unity, no more beauty" between his new robe and the rest of his belongings. So, he began to replace his old belongings with new ones that would equal the beauty of his robe. In the end, Diderot was surrounded by luxury, debt, and dissatisfaction. He bought things which he previously didn't need in order to feel happy or fulfilled.

The painting, "Diderot," by Louis-Michel van Loo, 1767

This story reveals our human nature and why it's so common for church leaders to spiral into feelings of inadequacy. We must lead from a place where we're secure in ourselves and confident in our leadership. At the same time, we must know our insufficiencies but rely upon God to be our sufficiency. Otherwise, we'll try to lead from a position of insecurity and place our confidence in other leaders who appear to be secure and confident—even if they are wrong—to supply us with what we think we need to compensate for our insufficiencies. We don't need to buy a new coat. We need to wear with confidence the coat we've been given.

God may very well direct us to move in rhythms like those we view as being on the front lines of leadership and to adopt similar leadership practices that mirror theirs. What God *requires*, however, is that we march to the beat of his heart. "His delight is not in the strength of the horse, nor his pleasure in the legs of a man, but the Lord takes pleasure in those who fear him, in those who hope in his steadfast love."[1]

When David faced Goliath, he didn't use Saul's upgraded battle equipment. He used a primitive slingshot to throw a rock and defeat a giant who had modern weaponry. David saved a nation with a slingshot. Gideon, along with one hundred men, didn't use horses, chariots, swords, and archers to defeat the army of Midian. He used jars, torches, and horns, and—similar to a birthday party prank—he turned on the lights and yelled, "Surprise!" Joshua didn't besiege Jericho to overthrow it. God had him organize a street parade, complete with a float and a marching band in uniform to lead the way, along with a silent procession of people marching behind to the music. All that they did was give a shout at the end of the parade route which decimated impenetrable walls and allowed them to capture a fortified city.

These leadership strategies are all quite different from what one would expect to be effective and innovative warfare tactics. Their unifying feature was that each of the leaders paid attention to *God's* leadership innovation and did what *he* directed them to do. Effective leaders are focused on conforming their leadership methods to the will of God and relying on his power. They aren't preoccupied with conforming to the philosophy of the predominating leadership group or the trends of the emerging leadership faction and the power that these external

---

1. Psalms 147:10-11 (NLT)

energies may produce. Leslie Allen in her book, *God of Stars and Broken Hearts*, said:

> Military power, the strength of cavalry and stamina of infantry, is a pale substitute, alien to the divine will from which God's people must take their cue (Hosea 1:7; Zechariah 4:6). Temptation to achieving power by such ways and fawning envy of those who possess such power (Ps 146:3) are false trails to success. The trust and worship of the faith community and patient waiting on Yahweh for covenant aid are qualities to be prized instead of an independent rush to arms or military alliance—that way madness lies (Isaiah 30:15-16; 31:1).

In this quote, Allen references Psalms 146:3 which, in the New Living Translation says, "Don't put your confidence in powerful people. There is no hope for you there." The only confidence we can truly have in leading our churches and ministries is knowing that we're obedient to God and are being true to ourselves. Whenever we look to the current in-group or the out-group for informational and normative cues, we're acting on our unconscious, innate nature, not on God's direction.

This has been a strategy that we've learned since humanity began to relate in groups. Whenever we look to God for those same cues, we're purposefully cultivating our openness to what I have termed *meditated exteriority directives*—that is, we're listening to God and being consciously sensitive to the explicit guidance or instructions coming from outside or beyond ourselves or from others.

If we feel that we must conform to the beliefs and behavior of the predominate culture of church leadership, or if we're only looking to do things differently, we may be justified in doing either of these based on the circumstances. There are times when we need to be doing what everyone else is doing. There are also times when we need to challenge the status quo. Regardless of either situation, the heart of the matter is that we must conform to the expectations God has for us to find and follow.

Admonishment #5: Be committed to what God has called you to do and how he has equipped you for his service and don't sidetrack yourself.

Questions:

- What are the beliefs you hold fast to that are resistant to compromise?
- When it comes to the influence that groups of people seem to exert on us, are you more likely to respond to their influence by going-with-the-flow or going-against-the-grain?
- Why is it so hard to do what God has given us to do in the way he has equipped us to do it rather than go along with what the methodologies and practices of the in-group?
- How has the Conformity bias affected you when it comes to your ministry and leadership?
- In what ways have you noticed the Diderot Effect creating the desire for you to upgrade areas of your ministry without pausing to consider if those areas are even in need of revision?
- What ministries or ministry leaders do you secretly observe for the purpose of upgrading your methods of ministry and leadership to reflect theirs?

CONCLUSION

Scripture records the name of only one son of Solomon who would be the successor to the throne after him.[1] It's likely that Rehoboam was the son who Solomon was thinking of when he was writing his ten soliloquies of wise instruction. Unfortunately, it's clear that Rehoboam didn't inherit the wisdom of his father. As evidenced by his leadership, it's doubtful that he was even paying attention to the instruction that his father was giving to him.

In 1 Kings 12, we read that as soon as Solomon died, the leaders of the twelve tribes came to Shechem to make Rehoboam the king of Israel. Because the people had been under heavy taxation to support the splendor of Solomon's kingdom, the leaders took this opportunity to express their complaint to Rehoboam in hopes that taxation might be lightened. Rehoboam asked for three days to consider the matter and to seek wisdom from his counselors.

He first sought the wisdom of the older men who had served as his father's counselors. They clearly had proven themselves to be men of wisdom. After all, they were advisors to the wisest man who had ever lived. These men of wisdom counseled Rehoboam to grant the request for taxation to be lightened so that the king might gain favor with the people. In doing so, they would become his servants forever.

---

1. 1 Chronicles 3:10; 1 Kings 11:43

Soliloquy № 7

Rehoboam then consulted with the young men who'd grown up with him and—from the advice that they gave him—clearly had no reputation for being wise. They advised him to tell the people, "My little finger is thicker than my father's thighs. And now, whereas my father laid on you a heavy yoke, I will add to your yoke. My father disciplined you with whips, but I will discipline you with scorpions."[1] The fact that Rehoboam took the advice of the younger men over the advice given to him by the older and wiser sages indicated the caliber of his mental capacity for evaluating wisdom. Ten of the twelve tribes instantly renounced their allegiance to Rehoboam, left for home, established a separate nation, and were forever lost to the house of David.

Perhaps you haven't given much thought to the five lessons that were presented in this book. Your currently-held position on these matters may be a result of heuristically-determined thought processes. Other influencers may be those seemingly-successful leaders who are also currently in church leadership somewhere and unconsciously serve as the source of your counsel. Many of these church leaders are likely to promote the popular position on the topics I have addressed but haven't taken the time themselves to think through their own heuristically-determined thought processes. I haven't been issued the responsibility of being the judge of their positions, but I have been given the responsibility to be the judge of my own.

And so have you.

This book has been written with the hope that it will be the voice of an older, wiser sage offering insight into other ways of thinking about these topics. I wanted to highlight some of the cognitive biases that we unknowingly succumb to that can keep us from thinking with wisdom. Perhaps you will reconsider your position on one or more of these areas—at the very least evaluate those people and thought processes that influence

---

1. 1 Kings 12:10-11

you and can inadvertently erode the effectiveness of your leadership. The aim of this book is to simply get you to *think* and to broaden the scope of your perspective so that you can be an effective leader in the Kingdom of God.

The Painting, "Rehoboam's Arrogance," by Hans Holbein, d.J., 1530

TERMS & DEFINITIONS

Admonish: To counsel (another) against something to be avoided or warn (that something is dangerous); To urge or exhort (someone to do something); To remind (someone) of something forgotten or disregarded, as an obligation or a responsibility.

Apophenia: The tendency to mistakenly look for connections and meaning between unrelated things to make sense of the world around us, often causing us to make mistakes in our correlations.

Architectural Determinism: The belief that architecture has the power to change people's behaviors in positive and predictable ways.

Black Swan Theory: Events that are rare, hard to predict, and beyond the realm of normal expectations which are often not taken into consideration when making predictions or attempting to determine outcomes.

Butterfly Effect: Term used to describe how macrosystems with too many factors at play (such as our daily lives) are prevented from being accurately predictable because of the many unpredictable microsystems that can influence outcomes.

Centrifugal: Moving away from a center: acting in a direction away from a center.

Centripetal: Moving toward a center: acting in a direction toward a center.

Combinatorial Explosion: Rapid growth that quickly reaches computational limits and occurs when small increases in the number of elements that can be combined increase the number of combinations to be computed.

Combinatorics: The branch of mathematics that deals with counting and combinations.

Conformity Bias: The tendency to behave similarly to the others in a group, even if doing so goes against your own judgment.

Diderot Effect: (most commonly used in consumerism) The effect a person experiences when they acquire something so superior in quality and style to an item they already own that this newly-acquired item immediately makes the current item it is replacing, along with all others used in the same context as the item, unacceptable.

Disciple building: The use of spiritual disciplines to exercise and progressively grow the faith of the interior spirit-man, of natural giftings to exercise and progressively grow in skill of the exterior natural-man, and the infilling of the Holy Spirit to empower the disciple.

Enclothed Cognition: The phenomenon of clothing being worn having a systematic influence upon the wearer's psychological processes, whereby enhancing psychological states, behavior, and performance.

Exponential Growth: Growth that occurs when the base number of something is multiplied.

Hedonic Adaptation: The general tendency for people to return to a preset level of happiness in spite of the ups and downs that life presents them with.

Hermeneutics: The branch of knowledge that deals with interpretation.

Ideogram: Pictures or symbols that represent not the object being pictured, but some thing or idea that the object pictured is supposed to suggest.

Illusion of Pundits: The confidence that comes with 20/20 hindsight, giving the appearance that one understands the past which fosters overconfidence in the ability to predict the future.

Linear Growth: Growth that consistently and steadily occurs by the same amount over time.

Meditated Exteriority Directives: When we're consciously sensitive to the explicit guidance or instructions that come from outside or beyond ourselves or others but rather, from God.

Prestige Bias: The tendency people have to look around and see others who are successful, study their behaviors and beliefs that don't conform to the dominant groups', and merely do what they do.

Pygmalion Effect: People will perform in ways that are consistent with the subtle expectations that leaders have of them.

Soliloquy: A type of extended speech that's not given directly to another person.

Specious: [spē'shəs] Having the ring of truth or plausibility but is actually fallacious; deceptively appealing.

Soliloquy № 7

Survivor Bias: Concentrating on the people or things that "survived" some process and inadvertently overlooking those that did not because of their lack of visibility.

Subtractive Epistemology: Knowledge that becomes illuminated by the removal of incorrect information rather than illuminated by the addition of correct information.

Superrational: Beyond the scope or range of reason.

Swimmer's Body Illusion: Occurs when we mistakenly believe that some result can be achieved by anyone as an outcome of participation when in reality there are selection factors of the individual that determine the results.

Via Negativa: A way of describing something by saying what it is not rather than by describing something by saying what it is. This is also known as "apophatic."

Appendix:
Cognitive Bias Charts

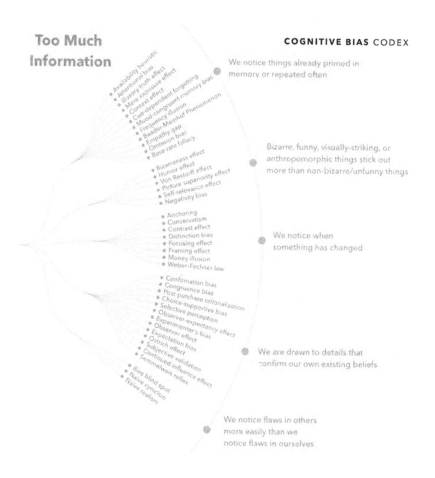

Soliloquy № 7

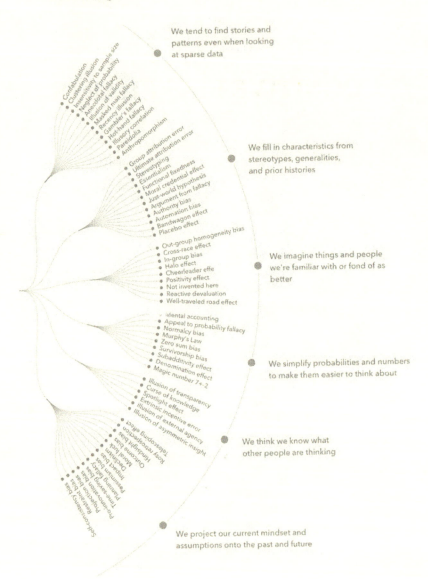

Appendix: Cognitive Bias Charts

COGNITIVE BIAS CODEX

**We Need
To Act Fast**

We favor simple-looking options and complete information over complex, ambiguous options

To avoid mistakes, we aim to preserve autonomy and group status, and avoid irreversible decisions

To get things done, we tend to complete things we've invested time & energy in

To stay focused, we favor the immediate, relatable thing in front of us

To act, we must be confident we can make an impact and feel what we do is important

- Less-is-better effect
- Occam's razor
- Conjunction fallacy
- Delmore effect
- Law of Triviality
- Bike-shedding effect
- Rhyme as reason effect
- Belief bias
- Information bias
- Ambiguity bias
- Status quo bias
- Social comparison bias
- Decoy effect
- Reactance
- Reverse psychology
- System justification
- Backfire effect
- Endowment effect
- Processing difficulty effect
- Pseudocertainty effect
- Disposition effect
- Zero-risk bias
- Unit bias
- IKEA effect
- Loss aversion
- Generation effect
- Escalation of commitment
- Irrational escalation
- Sunk cost fallacy
- Identifiable victim effect
- Appeal to novelty
- Hyperbolic discounting
- Peltzman effect
- Risk compensation
- Effort justification
- Trait ascription bias
- Defensive attribution
- Fundamental attribution error
- Illusory superiority
- Illusion of control
- Actor-observer bias
- Self-serving bias
- Barnum effect
- Forer effect
- Optimism bias
- Egocentric bias
- Dunning-Kruger effect
- Lake Wobegone effect
- Hard-easy effect
- False consensus effect
- Third person effect
- Social desirability bias
- Overconfidence effect

237

Soliloquy № 7

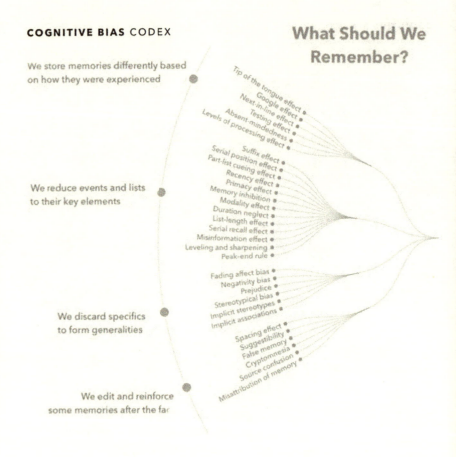

ACKNOWLEDGEMENTS

I would like to thank my dad [2.0], Eugene "Gene" Brown, for generously taking the time to help me with the painstaking task of editing and revising my manuscript. He was a tremendous blessing in helping me to prepare it for publication. His extremely sharp eyes, command of the English language, depth of knowledge of God's Word, and wealth of experience in both life and pastoral ministry were a tremendous help to me in ensuring that my theology was sound and that my thoughts were organized and communicated with clarity.

My wife, Christine, deserves a special thanks for being by my side and believing in me. She never batted an eye when I told her that I was thinking about writing a book, but only gave me the encouragement I needed for me to take my own thought seriously. (She was the first to give the book advanced praise even before there was ever a concept and before it was ever written.) Like Ruth in the Bible (who might have been a princess), she has humbled herself as a servant to "go where I go and lodge where I lodge," surrendering her plans over to God. God is going to bless her something special as she lays her crown at His feet and receives her reward in Heaven.

Finally, who would be here without their mom? Thanks, mom (Jane) for raising me to love the Lord, and for continually praying for me. You made me a disciple of Jesus.

A NOTE ON SOURCES

Opening Quotation:

Dickens, Charles. "Chapter Fifty–One: Sheds New and Brighter Light Upon the Very Dark Place; and Contains the Sequel of the Enterprise of Mr. Jonas and His Friend." In *Martin Chuzzlewit*. London: W. Barth, 1844.

INTRODUCTION

"Admonishment." In *The American Heritage Dictionary of the English Language*. Boston, MA: Houghton Mifflin Harcourt, 2011.

Arthur, Sarah. "What Is Story and Why Does It Work?" In *The God-Hungry Imagination: The Art of Storytelling for Postmodern Youth Ministry*, 78–87. Nashville, TN: Upper Room, 2007.

Desjardins, Jeff. "Every Single Cognitive Bias in One Infographic." Visual Capitalist, September 25, 2017. https://www.visualcapitalist.com/every-single-cognitive-bias/.

Elkin, Benjamin, and James Daugherty. *Gillespie and the Guards*. New York: Viking, 1967.

Lewis, C. S. "Sometimes Fairy Stories May Say Best What's to Be Said." In *On Stories: And Other Essays on Literature*, 47. San Diego, CA: Harcourt, 1982.

Machiavelli, Niccolò. *De Principatibus / Il Principe (The Prince)*. Italy:Antonio Blado d'Asola, 1532.

CHAPTER 1: THE OCEAN'S DEEP SECRET

"World War 2 Facts." World War 2, January 25, 2016. http://world-war-2.info/facts/.

Aird, Catherine. *His Burial Too*. Toronto, NY, London: Bantam Books, 1973.

Cicero, Marcus Tullius. "Book III." *M. Tullius Cicero of the Nature of the Gods; in Three Books. with Critical, Philosophical, and Explanatory Notes. to Which Is Added, an Enquiry into the Astronomy and Anatomy of the Antients*, 215. London: Printed for R. Francklin, in Covent-Garden, 1741.

Conner, Kevin J. *The Tabernacle of Moses*. Portland, OR: Bible Temple Publishing, 1976.

Chole, Alicia Britt. Choices: *To Be or Not to Be a Woman of God*. Onewholeworld, 1990. Cassette.

Collins, James C. *Good to Great: Why Some Companies Make the Leap—and Others Don't*. 1st ed. New York, NY: HarperBusiness, 2001.

Elton, Edwin J., Martin J. Gruber, and Christopher R. Blake. "Survivor Bias and Mutual Fund Performance." *The Review of Financial Studies* 9, no. 4 (October 1996): 1097–1120. https://doi.org/10.1093/rfs/9.4.1097.

Jewett, Robert. "Conflicting Movements in the Early Church as Reflected in Philippians." *Novum Testamentum* 12, no. 4 (1970): 362-90. https://doi.org/10.1163/156853670xx00063.

McRaney, David. "Survivorship Bias." *You Are Not So Smart*, May 23, 2013. http://youarenotsosmart.com/2013/05/23/survivorship-bias.

Smith, Gary. *Standard Deviations: Flawed Assumptions, Tortured Data and Other Ways to Lie with Statistics*. 1st ed. New York: Overlook, 2015.

Swete, Henry Barclay. *The Apocalypse of St. John: the Greek Text with Introduction Notes and Indices*. Eugene, OR: Wipf & Stock Publishers, 1998.

Taleb, Nassim Nicholas. *Antifragile: Things That Gain from Disorder*. New York, NY: Random House, 2012.

Wald, Abraham. "A Reprint of 'A Method of Estimating Plane Vulnerability Based on Damage of Survivors' by Abraham Wald." Alexandria: Center for Naval Analyses, 1980. 1-145. NC State University. http://www4.ncsu.edu/~swu6/documents/A_Reprint_Plane_Vulnerability.pdf.

CHAPTER 2: FASHION STATEMENTS

"Beauty with a Purpose: The Force Behind Native American Feathers." Indian Headdress. Novum Crafts, March 24, 2016. https://indianheaddress.com/blogs/news/99028422-beauty-with-a-purpose-the-force-behind-native-american-feathers.

"Christian Liturgy, V. Vestments and Liturgical Objects." In *Encyclopædia Britannica*, 14:129-135. Encyclopædia Britannica, 1973.

"Ideogram." In *Merriam Webster Dictionary*. Springfield, MA: G & C Merriam Co., 1981.

"Tail Wagging the Dog." Collins COBUILD Idioms Dictionary, 3rd ed. Farlex. Accessed February 28, 2020. https://idioms.thefreedictionary.com/tail wagging the dog.

"The Star Feathers: A Cherokee Legend." First People. Accessed February 19, 2018. http://www.firstpeople.us/FP-Html-Legends/TheStarFeathers-Cherokee.html.

They Live. Dir. John Carpenter. Prod. Larry Franco. Screenplay by (John Carpenter as) Frank Armitage. Perf. Roddy Piper, Keith David, & Meg Foster. Alive Films, 1988.

Adam, Hajo, and Adam D. Galinsky. "Enclothed Cognition." *Journal of Experimental Social Psychology*, vol. 48, no. 4 (July 2012): 918–925., doi:10.1016/j.jesp.2012.02.008.

Ahern, John J., "An Historical Study of the Professions and Professional Education in the United States" (1971). Dissertations. Paper 1158. http://ecommons.luc.edu/luc_diss/1158.

Barnhouse, Donald Grey. *The Invisible War: The Panorama of the Continuing Conflict Between Good & Evil*. Grand Rapids, MI: Zondervan Pub. House, 1965. 23.

Bernard, Katherine. "Confidence Dressing: How Clothing Affects the Mind." Vogue. Vogue, April 27, 2012. https://www.vogue.com/article/intelligent-design-how-clothing-affects-the-mind.

Bonazzo, John. "Sheryl Sandberg Educates, Mollifies Congress in Almost Perfect Testimony." Observer. Observer, September 5, 2018. https://observer.com/2018/09/sheryl-sandberg-mark-zuckerberg-jack-dorsey-congress/.

Cherry, Constance M. *The Worship Architect: A Blueprint for Designing Culturally Relevant and Biblically Faithful Services*. Grand Rapids, MI: Baker Academic, 2010.

Clemens, Samuel Langhorne, and Albert Bigelow Paine. *Mark Twain's Notebook*. New York, NY: Harper, 1935.

Cubberly, Ellwood P. *The History of Education: Educational Practice and Progress Considered as a Phase of the Development and Spread of Western Civilization*. Boston, MA: Houghton Mifflin, 1948. 189.

Darkholme, A. J. *Rise of the Morning Star*. 1st ed., vol. 1. Florida: Misterio Publishing, 2014.

Dent, Mark. "How the Power Suit Lost Its Power." The Goods. Vox, September 30, 2019. https://www.vox.com/the-goods/2019/9/30/20869237/suits-control-menswear-decline.

Flexner, Stuart Berg. "Perverse." In *Random House Unabridged Dictionary*. New York, NY: Random House, 1994.

Frederick, Shane, and George Loewenstein. "Hedonic Adaptation." *Well-Being: Foundations of Hedonic Psychology*. Plymouth: Rowman & Littlefield Group, 2003. 302-29.

Fuller, Thomas. *Gnomologia: Adagies and Proverbs; Wise Sentences and Witty Sayings, Ancient and Modern, Foreign and British*. B. Barker at the College-Arms near Dean's-Yard, Westminster; and A. Bettesworth and C. Hitch, at the Red-Lion in Pater-Noster Row: London, 1732. 65.

Fulwiler, Jennifer. "Why Don't We Dress Up Anymore?" National Catholic Register. EWTN News, Inc., June 27, 2012. http://www.ncregister.com/blog/jennifer-fulwiler/why-dont-we-dress-up-anymore.

Gilchrest, Andy. "Clothes DO Make the Man." Ask Andy About Clothes, February 5, 2018. https://askandyaboutclothes.com/clothes-do-make-the-man/. The latest research reports that when we encounter another human being that we notice the following about them in this order: 1. Skin color, 2. Gender, 3. Age, 4. Bearing – This includes height, head movement and body language, 5. Appearance, which includes the 90% of you covered in clothing, 6. Direct eye contact, and 7. Speech.

Greenwood, Ernest. "Professionalization." *The Elements of Professionalization*. Ed. Howard Vollmer and Donald Mills. Englewood Cliffs: Prentice-Hall, 1966. 10-17.

Grossman, Cathy Lynn. "Most Religious Groups in USA Have Lost Ground, Survey Finds." USA Today. Gannett Satellite Information Network, March 17, 2009. https://usatoday30.usatoday.com/news/religion/2009-03-09-american-religion-ARIS_N.htm.

Hartmans, Avery. "How to Dress like a Tech Billionaire for $200 or Less." Business Insider. Business Insider, May 6, 2018. https://www.businessinsider.com/clothes-worn-by-tech-billionaires-2018-5?op=1.

Hollie. "Let's Get Abstract with Simple Chinese Ideograms." Written Chinese, November 13, 2017. https://www.writtenchinese.com/lets-get-abstract-with-chinese-ideograms/.

Homer, and E. V. Rieu. *The Odyssey*. London: Methuen, 1952. (6.29-30, 242-3, 236-7).

Hooff, Johanna C. Van, Helen Crawford, and Mark Van Vugt. "The Wandering Mind of Men: ERP Evidence for Gender Differences in Attention Bias towards Attractive opposite Sex Faces." *Social Cognitive and Affective Neuroscience* 6.4 (2010): 477-85.

Hoy, David Couzens. *The Critical Circle: Literature, History, and Philosophical Hermeneutics*. Berkeley, CA: University of California, 1982.

Kane, Clare. "That Outfit You're Wearing May Be Affecting How You Think, Says Science." Mic. Mic, December 3, 2015. https://www.mic.com/articles/129502/that-outfit-you-re-wearing-may-be-affecting-how-you-think-says-science#.x8sHtHCMq.

Karl, Katherine A., Leda Mcintyre Hall, and Joy V. Peluchette. "City Employee Perceptions of the Impact of Dress and Appearance." *Public Personnel Management* 42, no. 3 (August 16, 2013): 452–70. https://doi.org/10.1177/0091026013495772.

Karlin, Lily. "TV Anchor Wears Same Suit for a Year to Prove Sexism is Going Strong." *The Huffington Post*. The Huffington Post, November 17, 2014. https://www.huffingtonpost.com/2014/11/17/tv-anchor-same-suit-sexism_n_6170900.html.

Klein, Karen E. "Dressed for Excess." Bloomberg.com. Bloomberg, January 8, 2001. https://www.bloomberg.com/news/articles/2001-01-08/dressed-for-excess.

Kraus, Michael W., and Wendy Berry Mendes. "Sartorial Symbols of Social Class Elicit Class-Consistent Behavioral and Physiological Responses: A Dyadic Approach." *Journal of Experimental Psychology: General* 143, no. 6 (2014): 2330–40. https://doi.org/10.1037/xge0000023.

Lawrence, Nathan. "The Law of the Fringes and You." *Hoshana Rabbah Blog*. March 31, 2013. https://hoshanarabbah.org/blog/2013/03/24/the-law-of-the-fringes/

Mcelhatton, Emmet and Brad Jackson. "Paradox in Harmony: Formulating a Chinese Model of Leadership." *Leadership*. 8, no. 4. (2012). 441-61. https://doi.org/10.1177/1742715012444054.

McKeever, Joe. "Does It Matter How the Preacher Dresses?" *Pastor Joe McKeever*. February 5, 2016. http://joemckeever.com/wp/matter-preacher-dresses/.

McRaney, David. *You Are Now Less Dumb: How to Conquer Mob Mentality, How to Buy Happiness, and All the Other Ways to Outsmart Yourself*. New York, NY: Gotham, 2014.

Murphy, Kate. *You're Not Listening: What You're Missing and Why It Matters*. New York, NY: Celadon Books, 2020. Pinsker, Joe. "Wearing a Suit Makes You Think Differently." *The Atlantic*. Atlantic Media Company, April 30, 2015. https://www.theatlantic.com/business/archive/2015/04/wearing-a-suit-makes-people-think-differently/391802/.

Quintilianus, Marcus Fabius, and Ferdinand Meister. *Institutio Oratoria*. Lipsiae: Freytag, 1886. (orat. 8 pr. 20).

Riesman, David. *The Lonely Crowd*. Yale University Press, 1969.

Roach, Joseph R. *It*. University of Michigan Press, 2007.

Roterodamus, Desiderius "Erasmus". *Adagiorum Chiliades*. Basileae: In Aedibus Ioannis Frobenii, Mense Octobri, 1508. (3.1.60).

Sarda-Joshi, Gauri. "7 Ways Your Clothes Change the Way You Think." Brain Fodder. Jeff Mann, June 17, 2016. https://brainfodder.org/psychology-clothes-enclothed-cognition/.

Sertillanges, A. D. "VIII. Creative Work, 3. Detachment from Self and the World." Trans. Mary Ryan. In *The Intellectual Life: It's Spirit, Conditions, Methods*. Westminster, MD: Newman, 1948. 153.

Sicinski, Adam. "How to Model Successful People and Develop the Mindset of a High Achiever." IQ Matrix Blog, December 10, 2018. https://blog.iqmatrix.com/model-successful-people.

Slepian, Michael L., Simon N. Ferber, Joshua M. Gold, and Abraham M. Rutchick. "The Cognitive Consequences of Formal Clothing." *Social Psychological and Personality Science* 6, no. 6 (2015): 661–68. https://doi.org/10.1177/1948550615579462.

Spurgeon, C. H., and David Otis. Fuller. "April 28, Evening." In *Morning and Evening: Daily Devotions*. Grand Rapids, MI: Zondervan Pub. House, 1948.

Taleb, Nassim Nicholas. *Antifragile: Things That Gain from Disorder*. New York: Random House, 2012. 322-324.

Twain, Mark. "The Czar's Soliloquy." *The North American Review*, vol. 180, no. 3, March (1905): 321-326. All words written or dictated by Samuel L. Clemens (Mark Twain) are in the public domain if they were first published before 1923.

Wagner, Laura. "What Sheryl Sandberg Wears to Work." Women.com, May 6, 2017. https://www.women.com/laurawagner/lists/what-sheryl-sandberg-wears-to-work.

Wang, Yajin, and Deborah Roedder John. "Louis Vuitton and Conservatism: How Luxury Consumption Influences Political Attitudes." Thesis. Marketing Department, Carlson School of Management, University of Minnesota, 2015. *Louis Vuitton and Conservatism: How Luxury Consumption*

Influences Political Attitudes. Institute for Brands and Brand Relationships, May 27, 2015. http://bbr2015.brandrelationships.org/wpcontent/uploads/sites/3/2015/05/Luxury-Consumption-and-Political-Attitudes_BBR_Yajin-Wang.pdf.

CHAPTER 3: ARCHITECTS OF THE ARCHETYPE

Introduction to Combinatorics. Khan Academy. Computer Animation on Khan Academy: A Collaboration between Pixar Animation Studios and Khan Academy. Sponsored by Disney, August 27, 2015. https://www.khanacademy.org/partner-content/pixar/crowds/crowds-1/v/intro-crowds.

"Mark & Luke." *The Pulpit Commentary.* Ed. H. D. M. Spence-Jones and Joseph S. Excel. Vol. 16. Grand Rapids, MI: Eerdmans, 1950.

Merriam-Webster.com Dictionary, s.v. "centrifugal," accessed April 17, 2020, https://www.merriam-webster.com/dictionary/centrifugal.

Merriam-Webster.com Dictionary, s.v. "centripetal," accessed April 17, 2020, https://www.merriam-webster.com/dictionary/centripetal.

The Pruitt-Igoe Myth: An Urban History. Dir. Chad Freidrichs. Prod. Paul Fehler, Chad Freidrichs, Jaime Freidrichs, and Brian Woodman. By Chad Freidrichs and Jaime Freidrichs. Unicorn Stencil, February 11, 2011. The Pruitt-Igoe Myth. 2011. http://www.pruitt-igoe.com.

"What Is the Butterfly Effect?" wiseGEEK. Conjecture Corporation, May 29, 2020. https://www.wisegeek.com/what-is-the-butterfly-effect.htm.

Al Shawa, Bashar. "The DARKER Side of Villa Savoye." *Misfits' Architecture*. September 3, 2011. https://misfitsarchitecture.com/2011/09/03/the-darker-side-of-villa-savoye/.

Allen, Michael R., and Nora Wendl. "The Unmentioned Modern Landscape." *Pruitt Igoe Now*. March 25, 2019. http://www.pruittigoenow.org/the-unmentioned-modern-landscape/.

Bair, Tor. "Exponential Growth Isn't Cool. Combinatorial Growth Is." *Medium*. Medium, December 28, 2015. https://medium.com/@TorBair/exponential-growth-isn-t-cool-combinatorial-growth-is-85a0b1fdb6a5.

Barnes, Albert. "Matthew Chapter 21." In *Notes on the New Testament: Explanatory and Practical*, edited by Robert Frew. Enlarged Type ed. Vol. 1. Grand Rapids, MI: Baker Book House, 1949.

Blair, Clay, Jr. *Silent Victory: The U.S. Submarine War against Japan*. New York, NY: Bantam, 1976. 1044.

Borland, Brad. "Size, Strength, or Power? A Training Method Primer." *Breaking Muscle*. April 2, 2018. https://breakingmuscle.com/fitness/size-strength-or-power-a-training-method-primer.

Broady, Maurice. "Social Theory in Architectural Design." *Arena: The Architectural Association Journal* 81 (1966): 149-54.

Dobeli, Rolf. "Does Harvard Make You Smarter?" In *The Art of Thinking Clearly*. London: Sceptre, 2013. 4-6.

Epstein, Isidore, and Joseph H. Hertz. Ed. Seder Nezikin. *The Babylonian Talmud*. Vol. 7. London: Soncino, 1935. Ser. 4.

Fairorth, Bennett Lear. *Dear Jon: Letters to and from a Former Teacher, 9-11-93 to 11-9-04*. New York, NY: IUniverse, 2005.

Farelly, Elly. "Bringing Home The 8 Million Boys After WWII; Operation Magic Carpet." *WAR HISTORY ONLINE*. September 21, 2017. https://www.warhistoryonline.com/world-war-ii/brining-home-8-million-boys-wwii-operation-magic-carpet.html.

Ganzel, Bill. "Labor Shortages." *Farm Labor Shortages during World War II*. March 25, 2019. https://livinghistoryfarm.org/farminginthe40s/money_03.html.

Gelertner, Mark. "Sources of Architectural Form: A Critical History of Western Design Theory" by Mark Gelernter, Manchester University Press, 1995, 300pp, 100 B&W Illus. Arq: *Architectural Research Quarterly* 1.03 (1996): 251.

Golembiewski, Jan. "Building a Better World: Can Architecture Shape Behaviour?" *The Conversation*. March 25, 2019. http://theconversation.com/building-a-better-world-can-architecture-shape-behaviour-21541.

Gyure, Dale Allen. Minoru Yamasaki: *Humanist Architecture for a Modernist World*. New Haven, CT: Yale UP., 2017.

Heylar, John. "Hooters: A Case Study." *Fortune*, September 1, 2003.

Ketcham, Christopher. "The Curse of Bigness." *Orion Magazine*. March 3, 2010. https://orionmagazine.org/article/the-curse-of-bigness/.

Kingsolver, Barbara. *Flight Behavior: A Novel*. New York: Harper, 2012.

Livingston, J. Sterling. *Pygmalion in Management*. Boston, MA: Harvard Business Review Press, 2009.

Longman, Tremper, Mark L. Strauss, and Daniel Taylor. "1 Thessalonians." *The Expanded Bible: Explore the Depths of the Scriptures While You Read*. Nashville, TN: Thomas Nelson, 2011.

Miller, Andrew. "Which Type of Growth Model Is Right for Your Business?" *Forbes*. Forbes Magazine, August 16, 2017. https://www.forbes.com/sites/forbesagency-council/2017/08/16/which-type-of-growth-model-is-right-for-your-business/#175476f97d2f.

Moore, Rowan. "Pruitt-Igoe: Death of the American Urban Dream." *The Guardian*. N.p., February 25, 2012. https://www.theguardian.com/artanddesign/2012/feb/26/pruitt-igoe-myth-film-review.

News Staff. "Clark Kent Was Right–With the Glasses, You Didn't Know He Was Superman." Scientific Blogging. Science 2.0, September 1, 2016. https://www.science20.com/news_articles/clark_kent_was_right_with_the_glasses_you_didnt_know_he_was_superman-179598.

Nowrasteh, Alex. "Post-World War II Migration and Lessons for Studying Liberalized Immigration." *Cato Institute*. January 28, 2014. https://www.cato.org/blog/post-world-war-ii-migration-lessons-studying-liberalized-immigration.

Steele, Billy. "Apple Acquires Beats Electronics for $3 Billion." *Engadget*. July 14, 2016. https://www.engadget.com/2014/05/28/apple-acquires-beats-electronics-for-3-billion/.

Taleb, Nassim Nicholas. *The Black Swan: The Impact of the Highly Improbable*. New York, NY: Random House, 2007. 109-110.

Thayer, Joseph and William Smith. "Greek Lexicon entry for Dunamis." *The NAS New Testament Greek Lexicon*. 1999.

Vaters, Karl. "Jesus And Crowds – An Unhappy Marriage." *Pivot / A Blog by Karl Vaters*. Christianity Today, June 28, 2017. https://www.christianitytoday.com/karl-vaters/2017/june/jesus-and-crowds-unhappy-marriage.html?start=1.

Heyer, Paul. *Architects on Architecture: New Directions in America*. New York, NY: Walker & Company, 1966. 186.

White, Ellen Gould "Opening the Door to the Adversary." *True Revival the Church's Greatest Need; Selections from the Writings of Ellen G. White*. Hagerstown, MD: Review and Herald Pub. Association, 2010. 12.

_____. "The Bible and the French Revolution." *The Great Controversy*. Mountain View, CA: Pacific Press Publishing Association, 1911. 267.

_____. "The Kind of Sermons Needed." *Testimonies to Ministers and Gospel Workers: Selected from Special Testimonies to Ministers and Workers*. Mountain View, CA: Pacific Press Publishing Association, 1923. 338.

CHAPTER 4: DESERT SAND THROUGH THE HOURGLASS

"Examples of Hindsight Bias." *YourDictionary*. June 23, 2016. https://examples.yourdictionary.com/examples-of-hindsight-bias.html.

The Living Nach: A New Translation Based on Traditional Jewish Sources. Vol. 3, Moznaim Publishing Corporation, 1994.

Buzzati, Dino. *The Tartar Steppe*. Trans. Stuart C. Hood. London: Secker & Warburg, 1952.

HaDarshan, Rabbi Shimon Ashkenazi. "Ruth." *Yalkut Shimoni: Midrash al Torah,Neviium u-Khetuvim*. Yarid ha-Sefarim, Jerusalem: 2006. 608.

Hurnard, Hannah. *Hinds' Feet on High Places*. Wheaton, IL: Living/Tyndale, 1975.

Kahneman, Daniel. "The Illusions of Pundits." *Thinking, Fast and Slow*. London: Penguin, 2012. 219-20.

Kitov, Eliyahu. "Sivan: Ruth & David." *The Book of Our Heritage: The Jewish Year and Its Days of Significance*. Trans. Nachman Bulman. Revised by Dovid Landesman & Joyce Bennett. 3rd ed. Vol. 3. Jerusalem: Feldheim, 1997. 819-64. Print. Originally published in 1962 in Hebrew as Sefer ha-Toda'ah.

Kohen, Šelomoh. "Vayeishev." *Siftei Kohen: Mahzor Li-teffilat šabbat*. Marakeš: n.p., 1646.

Minter, Deborah. "Facts of the Black Swan." *Owlcation*. Owlcation, December 23, 2017. https://owlcation.com/stem/Facts-of-the-Black-Swan.

Mo'ed, Seder. "Chapter V, 55b." *The Babylonian Talmud*. Trans. I. Epstein. Vol.Shabbath. London: Soncino, 1938. 256.

Neusner, Jacob. "Chapter 5: Folio 91a, Migration from the Land of Israel by Reason of Famine; the Case of Ruth's Family." *The Babylonian Talmud: A Translation and Commentary: Tractate Baba Batra*. Vol. 15. Peabody, Mass: Hendrickson, 2005. 271.

Nezkin, Seder. "Chapter XI, 105b." In *The Babylonian Talmud*. Trans. I. Epstein. Vol. Sanhedrin II. London: Soncino, 1935. 719.

Puhvel, Jaan. "The Origin of Etuscan Tusna ("Swan"). *The American Journal of Philology* 105.2 (1984): 209-12.

Seneca, Lucius Annaeus. *On the Shortness of Life*. Place of publication not identified: Lulu.com. 2017.

Starbuck, William H. et al. "Payoffs and Pitfalls of Strategic Learning." *Journal of Economic Behavior & Organization*, vol. 66, no. 1, August, 2008, pp. 7-21., doi:10.1016/j.jebo.2007.02.003.

Taleb, Nassim Nicholas. "Corporate Teleology." In *Antifragile: Things That Gain from Disorder*. New York, NY: Random House, 2016. 234-35.

_____. *Fooled by Randomness: The Hidden Role of Chance in Life and in the Markets*. New York, NY: Random House, 2001. 35.

_____. *The Black Swan: The Impact of the Highly Improbable*. New York, NY: Random House, 2007. xvii-iii.

Tetlock, Philip E. *Expert Political Judgement: How Good Is It? How Can We Know?* Princeton, NJ: Princeton UP, 2006.

CHAPTER 5: ALTOGETHER SEPARATE

"go against the grain." In *Cambridge Dictionary of American Idioms*. 2006. Cambridge University Press. November 1, 2016. http://idioms.thefreedictionary.com/go+against+the+grain

"go with the flow." In *Cambridge Dictionary of American Idioms*. 2006. Cambridge University Press. November 1, 2016. http://idioms.thefreedictionary.com/go+with+the+flow

"Nuremberg Race Laws: Translation." *United States Holocaust Memorial Museum*. United States Holocaust Memorial Council, July 2, 2016. https://www.ushmm.org/wlc/en/article.php?ModuleId=10007903.

"The Human Condition." *Prestige Bias*. December 25, 2014. http://humancond.org/analysis/bias/prestige.

"The Segelschulschiff Horst Wessel." *EXposureUSA: Nautical Sailing News*. October 28, 2016. http://www.exposureusa.org/sailing-ship-classifications/the-segelschulschiff-horst-wessel.

"Verbotene Liebe | Courage." *Die Forschungs- Und Arbeitsstelle »Erziehung Nach/über Auschwitz«*. Research and Study Center for Holocaust Education, October 29, 2016. http://fasena.de/courage/index.htm.

Allen, Leslie C. "God of Stars and Broken Hearts: God's Provision and Dependability." *Psalms 101-150*. Vol. 21. Grand Rapids, MI: Zondervan, 2015. 386.

Budanovic, Nikola. "This Man Refused to Salute Hitler, And Here Is Why." *WAR HISTORY ONLINE*. June 28, 2016. https://www.warhistoryonline.com/world-war-ii/this-man-refused-to-salute-hitler-and-here-is-why.html.

Diderot, Denis. "Regrets for My Old Dressing Gown, or A Warning to Those Who Have More Taste than Fortune." Translated by Mitchell Abidor. Regrets for my Old Dressing Gown by Denis Diderot 1769, 2005. https://www.marxists.org/reference/archive/diderot/1769/regrets.htm.

Eckler, Irene. *A Family Torn Apart by "Rassenschande": Political Persecution in the Third Reich*; Documents and Reports from Hamburg in German and English. Trans. Jean Macfarlane. Schwetzingen: Horneburg Verlag, 1998.

Emerson, Ralph Waldo. "Self-Reliance." *Essays: First Series.* Boston, MA: James Monroe & Company, 1841.

Nesov, Vladmir. "Conformity Bias." *LessWrong Wiki.* Machine Intelligence Research Institute, May 13, 2009. https://wiki.lesswrong.com/wiki/Conformity_bias.

Richerson, Peter J., and Robert Boyd. *Not by Genes Alone: How Culture Transformed Human Evolution.* Chicago, IL: U of Chicago, 2005.

Seneca, Lucius Annaeus, and Robin Campbell. "Letter IX." *Letters from a Stoic = Epistulae Morales Ad Lucilium.* London: Penguin Classics, 2014. 30-31.

_____. "Letter VII." *Letters from a Stoic = Epistulae Morales Ad Lucilium.* London: Penguin Classics, 2014. 17.

Vogt, Brent A. "Pain and Emotion Interactions in Subregions of the Cingulate Gyrus." *Nature Reviews Neuroscience* 6.7 (2005): 533-44.

ILLUSTRATION CREDITS

COVER IMAGE
"Rehabeams Übermut: Büste Des Königs Rehabeam (The Arrogance of Rehoboam: Bust of Rehoboam)" by Hans Holbein d. J., *Kunstmuseum Basel*, 1530, Sammlung Online, Basel, Switzerland. Used with permission.
Located at http://sammlungonline.kunstmuseumbasel.ch/eMuseumPlus?service=ExternalInterface&module=collection&objectId=1492&viewType=detailView. Fragment of the Painting on the Southern Wall of the Meeting Hall of the Great Council in the Basel Townhall. Tempera on lime plaster (al secco) 28 x 41.5 cm. Not inscribed. Kunstmuseum Basel Entrance between 1825 and 1833. Inv. 328.

> Hans Holbein the Younger was commissioned to paint the south wall of the Basel Council Chamber. The episode depicted was intended to serve as a warning to the Basel councilors of excessive severity: the Israelites ask Rehoboam, the son of King Solomon, for a lighter regiment than that of his father. On the contrary, when the heir to the throne threatens to tighten them, they turn away from him and thus from the house of David. The young counselors put the metaphorical words into Rehoboam's mouth that his

Soliloquy № 7

little finger is thicker than his father's waist (1 Kings 12:10).

TITLE PAGE IMAGE
"Coat of arms of the municipality of Sankt Stephan (Switzerland)" by Aliman5040; located at https://commons.wikimedia.org/wiki/File:Sankt_Stephan-coat_of_arms.svg. This work is licensed under the Creative Commons Attribution-ShareAlike 3.0 Unported License. To view a copy of this license, visit http://creativecommons.org/licenses/by-sa/3.0/ or send a letter to Creative Commons, PO Box 1866, Mountain View, CA 94042, USA. Permission is granted to copy, distribute and/or modify this document under the terms of the GNU Free Documentation License located at https://en.wikipedia.org/wiki/GNU_Free_Documentation_License, Version 1.2 or any later version published by the Free Software Foundation; with no Invariant Sections, no Front-Cover Texts, and no Back-Cover Texts. A copy of the license is included in the section entitled *GNU Free Documentation License* located at https://commons.wikimedia.org/wiki/Commons:GNU_Free_Documentation_License,_version_1.2.

> *The image is the Coat of arms of Sankt Stephan (St. Stephen), Switzerland, which is also the flag of that municipality. It depicts Stephen of Acts 6:8-7:59, holding a Bible in his right hand and a martyr's palm branch in his left while carrying a pouch of stones (he was stoned to death for denouncing the leaders of Israel for being stiff-necked and opposing the Holy Spirit, as recorded in Acts 7:51-53). A root of the author's family tree originates from this municipality in Switzerland.*

Illustration Credits

CHAPTER 1

"Survivorship-bias" by McGeddon; located at https://commons.wikimedia.org/wiki/File:Survivorship-bias.png. Illustration of hypothetical damage pattern on a WW2 bomber, dot pattern roughly based on that given at http://www.motherjones.com/kevin-drum/2010/09/counterintuitive-world which gives credit to Cameron Moll.

This work is licensed under the Creative Commons Attribution-ShareAlike 4.0 International License. To view a copy of this license, visit http://creativecommons.org/licenses/by-sa/4.0/legalcode or send a letter to Creative Commons, PO Box 1866, Mountain View, CA 94042, USA.

CHAPTER 2

"(gān) Sweet" by Andres Leo. Located at (http://www.chinese-word.com/data/3536.html). Used with permission.

CHAPTER 4

"Black Swan" by EllieRH; located at https://commons.wikimedia.org/wiki/File:Black_Swan_in_Australia.JPG. Black swan on waterhen lake in Oxenford, Gold Coast AU.

This work is licensed under the Creative Commons Attribution-ShareAlike 4.0 International License. To view a copy of this license, visit http://creativecommons.org/licenses/by-sa/4.0/legalcode or send a letter to Creative Commons, PO Box 1866, Mountain View, CA 94042, USA.

CHAPTER 5

"August Landmesser" by unknown author; located at https://commons.wikimedia.org/wiki/File:August-Landmesser-Almanya-1936.jpg. Picture of people giving a Nazi salute, with an unidentified person refusing to do so. Marked as public domain, more details on Wikimedia Commons: (https://commons.wikimedia.org/wiki/Template:PD-anon-70). This media file is in the public domain in the United States. This applies to

Soliloquy № 7

U.S. works where the copyright has expired, often because its first publication occurred prior to January 1, 1925, and if not then due to lack of notice or renewal.

"Portrait of Denis Diderot (1713-1784)" by Louis-Michel van Loo (1707-1771); located at https://commons.wikimedia.org/wiki/File:Louis-Michel_van_Loo_-_Portrait_of_Denis_Diderot_-_WGA13440.jpg. Marked as public domain, more details on Wikimedia Commons: https://commons.wikimedia.org/wiki/Template:PD-old. This media file is in the public domain in the United States. This applies to U.S. works where the copyright has expired, often because its first publication occurred prior to January 1, 1925, and if not then due to lack of notice or renewal.

CONCLUSION
"Rehabeams Übermut (The Arrogance of Rehoboam)" by Hans Holbein d. J., *Kunstmuseum Basel*, 1530, Sammlung Online, Basel, Switzerland. Used with permission. Located at http://sammlungonline.kunstmuseumbasel.ch/eMuseumPlus?service=ExternalInterface&module=collection&objectId=19440&viewType=detailView
Pen and brown ink, over preliminary chalk drawing, gray wash, watercolors, mounted Sheet: 22.5 x 38.3 cm. Kunstmuseum Basel, Kupferstichkabinett, Amerbach-Kabinett 1662 Inv. 1662.141

COGNITIVE BIAS CHARTS
"Cognitive Bias Codex" The Cognitive Bias Charts are a derivative of the original work "Cognitive Biases Codex" by Designhacks.co.; Categorization by Buster Benson; Algorithmic Design by John Manoogian III (JM3); Data by Wikipedia, located at (https://www.visualcapitalist.com/wp-content/uploads/2017/09/cognitive-bias-infographic.html). This work is licensed under the Creative Commons

Illustration Credits

Attribution-ShareAlike 4.0 International License. To view a copy of this license, visit http://creativecommons.org/licenses/by-sa/4.0/ or send a letter to Creative Commons, PO Box 1866, Mountain View, CA 94042, USA. The original chart was divided into separate images by Infomaniac at *Through the Looking Glass News* at (https://throughthelookingglassnews.wordpress.com/2018/01/05/cognitive-bias-codex-188-systematic-patterns-of-cognitive-deviation-defined/) under the same license as the original.

ABOUT THE AUTHOR

Christopher M. McGough
BA, Bible/Theology | MA, Christian Ministries

Chris McGough, MA, serves as a Professor on the faculty of the Theology & Global Church Ministries department at Evangel University where he teaches courses in youth ministry and church leadership. With over twenty-five years of full-time ministry experience, he has served on staff in both the church and on the university campus, ministering to young people in a pastoral role. A student of both biblical history and current culture, Chris is a lateral-thinking strategist whose aim is to prepare church leaders for a future of effective ministry. He enjoys life with his wife and two children in Springfield, MO.

Printed in the USA
CPSIA information can be obtained
at www.ICGtesting.com
LVHW111252030823
753911LV00001B/43